2008

The Elementary

Common Sense

of Thomas Paine

An Interactive Adaptation for All Ages

Mark Wilensky

Illustrations by Totie Richardson

SB

Savas Beatie

New York and California

Printed in the United States of America

Cataloging-in-Publication Data is available from the Library of Congress.

ISBN 13: 978-1-932714-36-4

10 09 08 07 06 05 04 03 02 01 / First edition, first printing

An earlier version of this book was privately printed by the author under the title *The Elementary Common Sense of Thomas Paine* (13 Stars Publishing, 2005; ISBN 0-9778425-0-9).

SB

Savas Beatie LLC
521 Fifth Avenue, Suite 3400
New York, NY 10175
Phone: 610-853-9131

Editorial Offices:

Savas Beatie LLC
P.O. Box 4527
El Dorado Hills, CA 95762
Phone: 916-941-6896
(E-mail) editorial@savasbeatie.com

Savas Beatie titles are available at special discounts for bulk purchases in the United States by corporations, institutions, home schooling, and other organizations. For more details, please contact Special Sales, P.O. Box 4527, El Dorado Hills, CA 95762. You may also e-mail us at sales@savasbeatie.com, or click over for a visit to our wonderful website at www.savasbeatie.com for additional information.

For Merrick

— my little rebel —

The promise of future generations
burns bright in your eyes and in my heart.

Thomas Paine, in a painting by Auguste Milliere

Table of Contents

Table of Contents (continued)

Section IV: Fourteen Activities for the Classroom, or Just for Fun!

Table of Contents (continued)

Section V: Thomas Paine in the British Press

Photos, illustrations, charts, and tables have been placed
throughout the book for the benefit of our readers.

Introduction

My decision to write this adaptation and put together the book you are now reading created a lot of consternation for me. The purist in me recoiled in horror at the thought of touching a single word of this historic document. But the educator half of me successfully argued (and believed) that introducing students at a young age to our historic source documents would help lead to a lifelong love of history and an active involvement in American life.

But reading historic documents isn't easy to do. Most of these documents are inaccessible for a variety of reasons, not the least of which is that they are often difficult to understand. I knew it would be wonderful for students to read and live history at an early age, and then delve even deeper as their understanding grew. What I needed was a "gateway" document to make this happen. This is, of course, what educators do: supply help up front and slowly remove that assistance once students get more independent in their learning. Hence *The Elementary Common Sense of Thomas Paine*—my answer to the question of how to help my students understand, appreciate, and begin to love American History as much as I do.

I. Thomas Paine's *Common Sense* is one of America's greatest founding documents. It is also one of the greatest persuasive essays ever written. If you are just starting to learn about American history, let's face it: it's also pretty darn hard to read these documents in their original form.

We were not alive when these documents were written—eating, sleeping, and experiencing these events day-by-day, week-by-week, year-by-year—so it is hard for us to get a real sense of how scary and crazy things really were during that time. What's more, these historic documents reference all kinds of things that were common knowledge back then, but can leave us befuddled or scratching our heads now.

II. *Common Sense* was a pamphlet written by Thomas Paine in 1775 (published in 1776) while incredible events were happening in Colonial America. Its publication had a tremendous impact on future events. Although Thomas Paine was born and raised in England, he didn't like it much. Growing up there, he experienced firsthand what it was like to live day in and day out under a king and a system of government that didn't recognize individual potential. Thomas also believed that Parliament and kings were unconcerned with how ordinary citizens lived, and unless you were lucky enough to be born in a "titled" or "elite" family, you had little hope of living a happy or full life.

Luckily, Thomas met Benjamin Franklin during one of Franklin's many stays in England. Ben suggested that Thomas sail to North America and write about injustices of life under a monarchy. Ben even wrote him a recommendation letter.

Early in 1774, Thomas Paine arrived in Colonial America in Philadelphia. He came when many in the thirteen colonies were extremely angry at Parliament and Lord North (the Prime Minister of England). Surprisingly, a majority of the colonists still liked King George III, and felt deeply loyal to him.

Paine immediately went to work writing for a new magazine. He wrote his opinions on a wide variety of issues, including the need for women's rights and abolishing slavery. But the one subject that Paine was absolutely obsessed with was the idea that all people were born with freedoms, and living under the English Constitution was not freedom.

III. By the time Paine's pamphlet *Common Sense* appeared, war had already broken out. A complete misjudgment of the colonists' anger triggered fighting at Lexington and Concord in April of 1775. Bunker Hill, the siege of Quebec, and conflicts around Boston, Massachusetts, followed. When war broke out, the city of Boston was under British military rule, which harshly taught the colonists a lesson in obedience. However, even though there had been fighting, the idea of complete independence from England was not really what most of the colonists and many of the representatives in the Continental Congress wanted. Much of the population was confident that the current situation was just a series of disagreements and misunderstandings between "the mother country and its children." Not only that, many believed that King George III would eventually agree that the colonists' demands for less meddling in colonial affairs was reasonable, and that he would step in and force parliament to address those concerns. When that happened, many believed, everyone could make up and go back to being loyal British subjects and making a living.

IV. Thomas Paine, however, made it personal.

Common Sense was a powerful weapon because he made the monarchy the target of his ferocious and well-reasoned arguments. Indeed, much of *Common Sense* is a direct written attack against kings in general, and George III in particular. Why do we have kings? Where did they come from? Why keep them? Paine's 46-page pamphlet tried to convince Americans that they were misplacing their anger at Parliament, when they really should be furious at King George III. If Paine could persuade the readers of *Common Sense* that the King was the real cause of the suffering in American Colonies, then citizens would unite into a cohesive voice for separation, independence, and liberty.

V. I really hope that this book helps spark your interest in the founding of our remarkable country, and that it will make you want to continue reading America's original founding documents. This is one of the most important ways for you to understand how amazing—and unique— America is in world history. This country was founded on ideas that did not really exist anywhere else in the world. Thousands of people played very different, but critical parts in America's beginning. It is scary to think that the absence of even one of those parts might have derailed our founding and resulted in no United States of America (think of it like a giant jigsaw puzzle).

More mind boggling, our Founding Fathers were ordinary people like you and me, with extraordinary beliefs in the common good for their fellow citizens and future American generations. Their story—our story—is the most exciting story I know.

Acknowledgements

I would like to offer my sincere thanks to the many people who offered words of encouragement that helped make this book a reality. And then, of course, there are those who went above and beyond. Totie Richardson, your consistent and positive encouragement was greatly appreciated. I am ever grateful to Marie Norby-Loud, David Perry, Judy Atwater, Nancy Olmore, Myra Wilensky, Ryan Lucas, Rick Dotson, John Yannacito, Michael Yannacito, Shandra Blosser, the Allen Family, Dick Roding, and Catherine Kent. An extra nod is due to Peggy Thiessen, a passionate teacher who confirmed to me early in my career that teaching never has to be formulaic.

I consider myself deeply fortunate to have found the extremely talented folks at Savas Beatie to publish *Common Sense*. Marketing Director Sarah Keeney offered tremendous suggestions for advancing this work and helped edit the final version. Graphic designer Jim Zach added artistic depth with the striking cover design. Val Laolagi, another Savas Beatie author, designed the cool website that goes hand-in-hand with this book. Finally, Director Theodore P. "Ted" Savas has proven to me that he has that great combination of vision and an intrepid explorer's spirit. He skillfully pushed this book and me to even loftier heights, and I appreciated his mentorship greatly.

Finally, I have long enjoyed speaking with Jayson Haberkorn, an excellent sixth-grade teacher. We frequently talk about new teaching ideas in our never-ending attempt to engage the unique and remarkable students we get every year. I'm certain both of us would have been rebels in colonial times.

Mark Wilensky
Arvada, Colorado

The Interactive Printing Press

*T*he *Elementary Common Sense of Thomas Paine* is, as its subtitle *An Interactive Adaptation* implies, more than your typical words-on-a-page book. The idea of linking the book to a dynamic website came from the publisher, which has successfully produced a wide variety of titles that allow readers to access more information, trivia, facts, photos, and content on the Internet.

Those wishing to do so by using this book (and I hope that is everyone!) will find all the additional content on my website at www.newcommonsensebook.com.

Scattered throughout this book are entries tagged with a small printing press graphic:

If you see this icon, it means more information on this and related topics is available at my website at **www.newcommonsensebook.com**. I believe that the interactive aspect of this book is an important and helpful way to provide additional information that can be updated at any time. To the best of my knowledge, no other history book like this one combines the traditional book world with the new and unlimited world of the Internet in such an exciting and dynamic manner.

You may easily access this information by clicking on the large printing press icon below the navigation buttons on the left side of the website.

Directions for accessing "The Printing Press" . . .

1. Locate a printing press icon inside *The Elementary Common Sense of Thomas Paine*;

2. Click over to **www.newcommonsensebook.com**;

3. Locate and click on the "The Printing Press" graphic on the left side of the main home page;

4. You will be prompted to enter a <u>username</u> and <u>password</u>. The <u>username</u> is the thirteen-digit ISBN number of this book, which is: 9781932714364. This is already filled in for you on the site;

5. The <u>password</u> is the page number on which the icon is found. For example, if there is a printing press icon on page 65, you would enter that number in the space provided.

Once you unlock The Printing Press, we sincerely hope you enjoy the extra content I have provided as way of saying thank you for your support of my work and for learning your American history! I will continually update this section, so check back often.

While visiting my website, please take a few minutes to look around and familiarize yourself with it. The site is regularly updated with news about the the book, myself and special events, colonial news, and much more.

And don't forget to take part in the treasure hunt to win free signed books for your school library and other cool things.

What treasure hunt, you ask?

Ah, you have to look at the website and find the clues for yourself! That, after all, is one of the best ways to learn, right?

SECTION I:

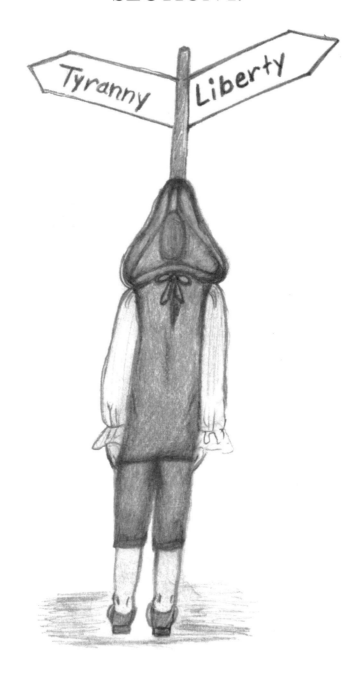

Thomas Paine

he author of *Common Sense* was born on January 29, 1737, in Thetford, England. He dropped out of school at an early age and tried working with his father, a staymaker, without much success. After a brief stint at sea, he worked as a taxing officer for the Crown, but was discharged in 1765 for neglect of his duties. Three years later he was appointed to a similar post in Sussex, where he engaged in the debates of a local political (Whig) organization. In 1772, Paine wrote the pamphlet *The Case of the Officers of Excise*, in which he argued for an increase in pay. He was dismissed for absence without leave two years later.

Accounts differ why Paine left England for the colonies, but after losing his child and first wife in childbirth, going bankrupt, and being divorced from his second wife, it was probably time to take a dramatic risk and start a new life. Paine arrived in Philadelphia racked with fever. He was left on board the ship in quarantine with other ill passengers. When a packet of letters written by Benjamin Franklin was found on Paine, the ill man was hoisted off ship and treated ashore in good accommodations.

In 1776, he published *Common Sense*, a powerful argument for American Independence. The pamphlet was widely read and helped encourage popular opinion in favor of independence from the Crown. Paine served in the Patriot army and wrote another pamphlet called *The Crisis* (1776-83), which boosted military morale.

Instead of remaining in America to help build the new country, Paine sailed back to Europe. There, he worked on inventions and pursued his writing. In support of the bloody French Revolution, he wrote *The Rights of Man* (1791). That, coupled with his previous works, branded him with the label of criminal in England for his anti-monarchist views. Paine avoided arrest by fleeing to France to join the National Convention.

The law finally caught up with Paine in 1793, when he was imprisoned in France for not publicly supporting the execution of Louis

XVI. While in prison Paine wrote and distributed the first section of one of his most controversial works called *The Age of Reason* (1794-96). Thanks to the efforts of James Monroe (the U.S. Minister to France) and others, Paine narrowly escaped the guillotine and walked away a free man in 1794. He remained in Napoleonic France until 1802, when Thomas Jefferson invited Paine to return to America. To his dismay, Paine discovered that his anti-religious views hurt his image in America, where his mighty contributions to the triggering of the American Revolution had been downplayed or ignored.

With few friends and unappreciated by the public at large, Paine died in New York City on June 8, 1809. He was 72 years old.

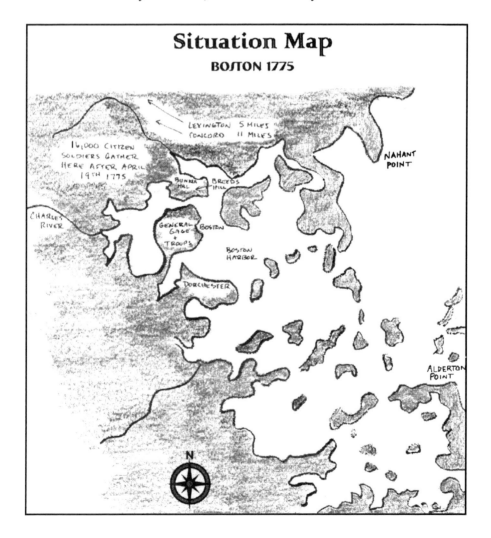

Situation Map
BOSTON 1775

Some Important Events Leading to Common Sense

❑ **1740**: Parliament passes laws permitting citizenship to people who have lived in the colonies for seven years. It also lets any citizen of the colonies carry his or her citizenship from colony to colony. A sense of togetherness in the colonies is created.

❑ **1760**: George III becomes England's king after the death of his grandfather, King George II, courtesy of hereditary succession.

❑ **1754–1763**: French and Indian War (or in Europe, the Seven Years' War). A land disagreement between the French in North America and the colonists brings British Regular Troops to the colonies. Colonial militias fight alongside the troops. Although Britain and its American colonies win the war, colonists are put off by the obvious arrogance exhibited by British commanders toward them. Colonists also learn firsthand how little the "titled elite" of England think of them. Many in Britain consider Americans to be second class English citizens and of peasant class, incapable of defending themselves.

❑ **1763**: The Royal Proclamation of 1763 gives the western lands (west of the Appalachians) back to the Indians and bans colonial settlement there. This is a big deal because a war was just fought to claim this land. The future growth of the colonies is again in doubt. Although this law is soon changed, colonists grow suspicious of England.

❑ **1764** (April): The "Sugar Act": A tax on sugar and other items that has a big impact by negatively affecting several markets with which the colonies trade.

❑ **1764**: The "Currency Act" prohibits the American colonies from issuing their own paper money in any form.

❑ **1765** (March): "Stamp Act." Colonists are angry because they are not part of Parliament and have no vote or say in such things as the passage of the Sugar Act. This is also seen as an attempt to restrict the many newspapers in the colony, as well as other freedoms Americans enjoy. "No Taxation without Representation!" begins to be heard.

❑ **1765** (March): "Quartering Act." Parliament requires colonists to allow British troops to stay in their homes, if needed. (See the text of the Quartering Act on page 71.) If this happens, the colonists must supply the troops with food ("victuals & cider").

❑ **1765** (October): Representatives from nine colonies gather and draft a petition to King George III stating that only colonial legislatures have the power to tax the colonists.

❑ **1766** (March): "Declaratory Act." Parliament says it can make laws for the colonies as needed, and the colonies must follow them.

❑ **1766** (August): The New York Legislature is suspended by English authorities after it refuses to enforce the Quartering Act.

❑ **1767** (June): "Townsend Acts." The Stamp Act is a complete failure and is canceled. But paint, paper, glass, lead, and tea are now taxed as they arrive in the colonies. The decision angers the colonists.

❑ **1768** (February): "Massachusetts Circular Letter." Samuel Adams writes a statement attacking Parliament's determination to continue taxing the colonies, while the colonies have no voice in Parliament. Adams calls for unification of the colonies. Many colonies accept the idea and write their own letter saying much the same thing.

❑ **1768** (September): English warships sail into Boston Harbor and English Infantry move into Boston to "keep order."

❑ **1769** (March): After defying recent parliamentary acts, the Virginia House of Burgesses is dissolved by the Royal Governor. The House of Burgesses was the first legislature in the English colonies. It first met in Jamestown, Virginia, in 1619.

❑ **1770** (March 5): "The Boston Massacre." British troops stationed in Boston are paid little and many spend their evenings looking for part-time work. Tensions have been high since they arrived in Boston, and the colonists are incensed by their attempts to take local jobs. Fights break out that eventually lead to the "massacre."

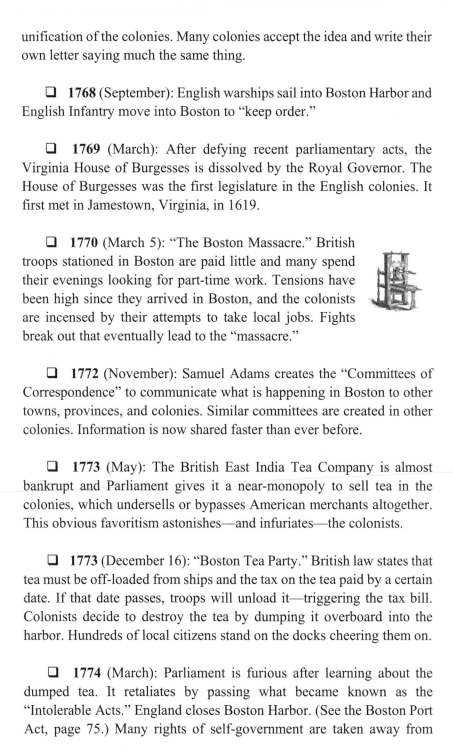

❑ **1772** (November): Samuel Adams creates the "Committees of Correspondence" to communicate what is happening in Boston to other towns, provinces, and colonies. Similar committees are created in other colonies. Information is now shared faster than ever before.

❑ **1773** (May): The British East India Tea Company is almost bankrupt and Parliament gives it a near-monopoly to sell tea in the colonies, which undersells or bypasses American merchants altogether. This obvious favoritism astonishes—and infuriates—the colonists.

❑ **1773** (December 16): "Boston Tea Party." British law states that tea must be off-loaded from ships and the tax on the tea paid by a certain date. If that date passes, troops will unload it—triggering the tax bill. Colonists decide to destroy the tea by dumping it overboard into the harbor. Hundreds of local citizens stand on the docks cheering them on.

❑ **1774** (March): Parliament is furious after learning about the dumped tea. It retaliates by passing what became known as the "Intolerable Acts." England closes Boston Harbor. (See the Boston Port Act, page 75.) Many rights of self-government are taken away from

Massachusetts. British soldiers who commit crimes get to go back to England for trial, and some Canadian boundaries are changed, which affects New England colonial borders. In addition to all this, the Quartering Act is expanded. (See Quartering Act on page 71.)

❑ **1774** (May): General Thomas Gage is appointed as martial law governor (civil laws, rights, and liberties are canceled and the military has direct rule) of Massachusetts. It becomes his job to enforce the closing of Boston Harbor.

❑ **1774** (May): Several colonies propose the idea of a Congress to discuss united resistance against the "Intolerable Acts."

❑ **1774** (September 5): The First Continental Congress meets. This is considered an act of treason by England.

❑ **1774** (September): "Powder Alarms." British General Gage hopes to avoid war by seizing gunpowder and other military supplies being gathered by colonists. Gage sends troops to raid Charlestown and seize weapons stored there. Many are alarmed that war might have started and they were caught unprepared for it. Colonists become more careful and keep a closer eye on British Regular Troops housed in Boston.

❑ **1775** (February): "New England Restraining Act." The New England colonies are now required to trade with England only, banning trade with other countries. Fishing in the North Atlantic is banned as well. (See Mercantilism, page 65.)

❑ **1775** (April 19): Lexington & Concord. General Gage again attempts to send soldiers to seize colonial military supplies. Paul Revere, William Dawes, and many others ride off to warn the local population. The "Shot Heard Around the World" (symbolically considered the first shot fired in the American Revolution) is fired on Lexington Green. After a sharp fight at Concord, several hundred American and British troops are killed and wounded as the Crown's soldiers retreat in disorder back to Boston. The "unthinkable" has to be reported to King

George III: Americans have fired on His Majesty's troops. American militia groups begin to gather outside Boston and surround the British camped within the city. Eventually, there will be as many as 16,000 citizen soldiers from several colonies gathered together.

❑ **1775** (May 10): The Second Continental Congress meets.

❑ **1775** (June 15): Congress creates the "Continental Army" from citizen soldiers around Boston and name George Washington as its commander.

❑ **1775** (June 17): Battle of Bunker Hill (which was actually fought on Breed's Hill). Concerned that more British soldiers were landing in Boston, colonial soldiers take action and build a redoubt (small fort) across the bay. The British attack it almost immediately. Although Americans are eventually driven back, the British suffer enormous losses, including many valuable combat officers.

❑ **1775** (July 8): The "Olive Branch Petition" is sent to England by Congress. This is a final attempt to "patch things up" with England. King George III ignores it and declares the Americans to be in rebellion. The King's words will not reach the colonies until January 1776. (See the Olive Branch Petition on page 85, and a Proclamation, by the King, for Suppressing the Rebellion & Sedition, page 98.)

❑ **1775** (Summer): Continental Congress appoints representatives to create peace treaties with neighboring Indian tribes.

❑ **1775** (September – November): Benedict Arnold leads 700 colonial soldiers up the Kennebec River (in what is today the state of Maine) and attacks British forces in Quebec, Canada. He is joined by Richard Montgomery, who guided soldiers up through Lake Champlain. Arnold hopes the attack will inspire local citizenry in Canada to rise up against the British, thereby drawing British forces away from America. The gamble does not work and the Americans are decisively defeated.

❏   **1775** (October 18): English ships attack Falmouth, Maine (Portland waterfront) and burn it to the ground. Maine was still part of Massachusetts at this time.

❏   **1776** (January 10): *Common Sense* is published just as news arrives that King George III had declared the colonies to be in rebellion. This means thousands of additional British Regular troops will arrive at the end of winter to "put down" the rebels. As the weeks pass, *Common Sense* becomes the largest selling pamphlet in American history.

It is still 176 days until the Declaration of Independence!

*   *   *

A Simplified Look at England's Government in 1775		
Parliament		
House of Commons	House of Lords Plus Prime Minister	KING
No Colonial Representatives	Lord North	King George III
Lower house of Parliament. Represents those without noble rank, influence, or title. Represents the common estates and local community.	The upper house of Parliament. Representatives are appointed, not elected, from among the senior and powerful nobles in Great Britain. Represents the elite estates and advises the King.	Monarch. The head of England. The supreme ruler of the empire

Chapter 1

The General Beginnings and Designs of Government and the Truth about the English Constitution

* * *

The Elementary Common Sense of Thomas Paine

Addressed to the Inhabitants of America

Some writers confuse us by not identifying the difference between a society and a government. Society is all the relationships between humans you see everyday. People who have the same interests, enjoy going to the same places and have common jobs and activities. The people you see at your school or play at your park. It's people with generally the same culture.

Governments are created by a society to establish rules and laws. If a government is designed well, some of our behaviors are restricted, but we can all probably agree that rules and laws are needed. We even pay for this government and these rules with our own money called taxes. So, government and society are closely connected but are really two different things.

But sometimes the people that become in charge of governments create misery for those who they are suppose to protect, creating a society that does not feel safe and secure. This is when the differences between the society we share with others and the government that rules that society becomes obvious.

To give you a clear idea of just what government should do for people, imagine you are among a small group of people that becomes stranded on a deserted island. You will be the first people in a brand new country. At first, you have no rules and that seems like a very good thing. You all would probably agree that everyone gets an equal portion of land, food, and water. However, to survive, you will all have to work together and use the skills of one another to hunt, collect food, and build shelters. Your small group of people will become a new society on this deserted island. Just like in school, you might find that some members of the group will work harder or have better skills than others.

However, what if a stronger member of the group decided to bully you and the others to get a bigger share? Or, members of the group start to disagree on who should live where, or how many trees should be cut down. More seriously, what if several people decided they couldn't get along with the others and decided to leave, by moving to another part of the island? Soon, the entire group starts to fall apart.

Logically, before really big problems start to happen, your group would meet and decide that something should be done. It is natural then, to form a government to create rules and laws to help the group stay and work together and settle differences.

*S*o, you all meet under a large tree in the middle of the island, and discuss what the "rules and regulations" of your society will be. Everyone is allowed to give their opinion, and decisions are made about rules, and consequences for breaking the rules. Your government is now growing from your island society. With hard work and luck, this government helps keep your society strong, safe, and working together.

*W*hat if more people get stranded on your island and your society grows? Will it become harder for all these people to agree on rules and punishments? Working together will also become more difficult, because as the population grows, people are moving farther and farther away from each other to find their own land on the island. Soon, the meetings under the tree cannot possibly be attended by EVERYONE on the island. There would be too many people. So, those living on all areas of the island (the mountain, the beach, the jungle…) could choose and send a **representative** to the meetings under the tree. These representatives would be expected to speak for and make decisions for the people who chose them.

> **Representative:** a person who speaks or acts for another or others.

*O*ur colonies continue to grow. With growth, concerns grow as well. There are more things to manage, more problems that occur, and more people and property to protect. As more property is added to the colonies, the farther apart we become, and the distances that citizens must travel to meet with one another becomes greater. These distances make it harder to meet with others and discuss appropriate laws and rules.

*Y*et, citizens' staying involved in their government creates common bonds with citizens from every part of the community. They will want to support and help each other because this benefits them all. The value of the government, and the happiness of its people who are governed, depends on the participation of citizens.

*G*overnment should be simple because the simpler any thing is, the less likely it is to be disordered, and it will be easier to repair when it does get out of order. A perfect government is one that costs the least and does the most. A government should represent the wants and needs of the society that created it and who lives under its protection. A government for the people, by the people.

* * *

*O*ur present system of government is NOT simple. When it was created long ago, it was good for people of that time because there was lots of **chaos** and **tyranny**.

> **Chaos:** total confusion.

*T*he **constitution** of England is so complicated and so confusing; people can suffer for years before other people can even figure out what needs to be fixed! It is almost impossible to find problem solvers who can even agree on what needs to be fixed.

> **Tyranny:** when government has absolute power over its citizens (often when power is held by one ruler).

> **Constitution:** a written document with the principles and laws of a country.

*T*he English government of 1775 is a jumbled mix of rules and laws from tyrannical kings, nobles, and commoners (the three branches of Parliament). To say that the constitution of England is a union of three powers, equally checking each other, is farcical, either the words have no meaning, or they are flat contradictions.

Paine believed that the English Constitution was very confusing.

The king and the peers do not create laws that give commoners freedoms. The commoners are supposed to be able to **check** the power of a king, but the king can reverse the process and block the power of the commoners. Any power the commoners have is an illusion. The government is clogged with ways to try and stop the power of a king, but useless, because the king's power is so broad, deep-rooted and forceful.

> To **Check** a government's power means to limit or stop parts of a government from becoming "all" powerful over its citizens.

Paine believed that Parliament was a house divided against itself.

*K*ings are shut off from the world, yet they create the laws that affect the world.

*Y*ou could describe the English government as:

The King, his friends and his family,

And

The commoners, which is everyone else.

This is a house divided against itself!

*W*ise people could not have designed this government! To give power to kings…..and then have citizens who are unable trust them? The whole situation is an act of planned self-destruction!

*W*e in America have been smart to use our distance from this absolute monarchy to add more freedoms to our lives, but we have given the key to the **Crown** to unlock the door and take those freedoms away!

*S*ince the fate of Charles I, it has proven dangerous for English Kings to look like they are trying to pass unpopular laws. To disguise these attempts at taking our freedoms, kings have become more careful by making it appear like it is Parliament's idea.

King Charles I upset a lot of people. He was beheaded in 1649, and monarchy was eliminated.

In 1660, Monarchy was restored.

Is Parliament restricting freedoms, or are kings
making the decisions and just hiding
behind Parliament?

The Main Points of Chapter One

☐ Paine wants to convince us that the laws of the British Government are very confusing and that kings are given way too much power. Government should be simple, designed by people working together, with laws that are designed to keep society safe and strong.

☐ Eighteenth century Parliament (the British government) is divided into three sections. The first is the king (monarch), who is the supreme ruler over the land. The second level of government is the House of Lords (the gentry or aristocracy). They are appointed, very wealthy, and own a great percentage of the nation's property. A majority of their wealth has been passed down from generation to generation. The third body is the House of Commons. This level represents the rest of the citizens and is suppose to work somewhat like a democracy. Each section is believed to keep an eye on the other two. However, Paine argues that because power in two of the three branches are passed down from one generation to the next (hereditary succession), how could this system possibly work?

☐ Paine says the current system only pretends to represent its citizens, but does not. It is a tangled system of "Haves and Have Nots," and that the king truly has all the power. Paine argues that government shouldn't have any power, unless it is granted to them by the people.

Chapter 2

Of Kings and Inherited Power

*T*here was a time in early history when Mankind was equal with one another. This equality could only have been destroyed by a later event or happening. What could have created this split?

*W*e might be able to understand the difference between the rich and the poor, but how did the world create greed and **oppression**?

ppression is created by people who want riches, yet when oppression is created, it rarely creates riches. And while **avarice** will protect an oppressor from being very needy or poor, it generally makes him too nervous of being rich.

> **Oppression**: The unjust or extreme use of power to take away individual rights.

> **Avarice**: greedy, the never-ending desire for wealth.

ut there is another difference, and this is the biggest difference there is, because there is no natural or religious reason that exists for this to happen: King and **Subjects**. What created this difference? To become a king, what makes them so special? Why is a king automatically "better" than us? This question is worth investigating.

> **Subjects:** person(s) under the authority or control of a monarch.

n early books, it is written that there were no kings and there were no wars. It is the pride of kings that throws mankind into confusion. Holland does not have a king and it has enjoyed more peace in the last hundred years than any of the European countries with kings.

e have allowed the descendants of the evil monarchy the very same power! Monarchy, in every instance, is one **tyrant** and everyone else who are required to worship him. Being a subject to the present king is degrading and shameful to ourselves, so to allow the next descendant to claim power over us as a matter of right . . . is an insult to us and our descendants.

> **Tyrant**: an absolute ruler who is not concerned with laws or the Constitution.

erhaps there is a king who has honor, honesty, and is well thought of by his generation. However, his descendants might be too worthless to

This is called Hereditary Succession . . . when a ruler's child or relative is automatically the next ruler.

inherit those same qualities. It seems ridiculous that any community could agree to one ruler who should **reign** over us and our children forever and ever. But then, to agree and believe that the Ruler's children should rule our children forever and ever! Ridiculous! Nature does give us "an ass for a lion" frequently.

Reign: to preside over subjects, usually with complete, unrestricted political power.

An ass for a lion? What if the King's son is not all that . . . "regal?"

*M*ost wise people treat inherited power with hatred. Because, once hereditary succession has begun, it is not easily removed. Many people are too scared, others are superstitious (they believe its bad luck to change), and there are those who share the wealth and power with the king and profit from this system.

*   *   *

*E*verything said so far would only refer to a present lineage of kings in the world if they happened to have had an honorable origin! But if we look deeper and trace the history of kings, in most cases we find someone no better than the head bully of a gang of thieves and plunderers, who probably became head of the gang because of savage manners, or an ability to influence the weaker minded, or overpowered the defenseless.

*U*nfortunately, there are very few records, or none at all, from those early days, so tall tales, urban legends, superstitions and lies have created stories and reasons that keep a king and his family in power, generation after generation.

Quotes from History

"What is history but a fable agreed upon?"
— **Napoleon Bonaparte**

---

*   *   *

*E*ngland has had a few good **monarchs**, but unfortunately, a much larger number of bad ones. The worst was William the Conqueror (1066CE) who sailed over from France with his gang of bullies and forced himself on England as king.

Monarchs: people who rule over a kingdom or empire, supreme rulers.

here are those weak minded people who worship the idea of heredity, but I doubt I could change their weak minds.

owever, I ask them this…How do they think the first kings came into power?! There are really only 3 ways:

Were kings chosen by lot? Probably not.

$\mathcal{B}$y lot (drawing straws?). If this were true, then there would be a pattern of drawing straws through history to produce the next king;

$\mathcal{V}$oted in. If the first King were voted in, then there would be a pattern of voting through history to produce the next king.

> **Usurpation:** to take something without legal authority.

$\mathcal{U}$surpation. Look to William the Conqueror! He was an usurper, there is no doubt!

William the Conqueror
England 1066- CE
9:30 a.m.

Oh crap...

How to Impose

William the Conqueror came over from France in the year 1066 and violently made himself king of all England. Paine says this was the true, and dishonorable, beginning of the monarchy.

$\mathcal{M}$en who look upon themselves as born to rule, and who believe that everyone else is to obey them, soon grow **insolent**. Being "elevated above all others," they start acting very differently from others. They lack the understanding of the needs and ambitions of the world outside themselves.

nother evil: a king dies young, so their child takes the throne. Youngsters can be taken advantage of, or betrayed. On the other hand, a king can grow old and crazy, and the very same can happen. In both these cases the public becomes the victim to every **miscreant** out there that could influence or counsel the king.

> **Insolent:** overbearing, insulting, arrogant and full of themselves.

> **Miscreant:** troublemaker

Quotes from History

"A man wrapped up in himself makes a very small bundle."

— Ben Franklin

---

*   *   *

t has been said that having the same family always rule (hereditary succession) saves a country from **civil wars**. LIES! Since William the Conqueror, England has had eight civil wars and 19 **rebellions**. For example, "The War of the Roses" (1422 to 1459) covered England in blood for many years.

> **Civil Wars:** a war between conflicting groups of citizens of the same country.

f we really investigate the daily tasks of a king, they accomplish little—generally leaving the next king in line to deal with the same useless goals or lack of goals.

orse, in **absolute monarchies**, the king is in charge of most everything; business, the military, and civil. They don't fill out an

Can young kings be taken advantage of by "trusted" advisors?

application to be king. It doesn't matter if they have no experience as a general, a judge or a commoner . . . kings often come un-experienced.

he pride of English government is imagined. Citizens believe that the Commoners, who are "elected" to parliament, help guide the country and look out for everyone. But it is an illusion; kings have eaten away these false liberties until they are just window dressing.

Why is the constitution of England sickly? Monarchy has poisoned the nation! The crown has overwhelmed the commons! In summary, monarchy and hereditary succession have covered the world in blood and ashes.

In England, this is very close to what the king really only does . . .

One: Make war and send his citizens to die.

Two: Give away places when the war goes badly.

A pretty good deal for a man to earn 800,000 Sterling a year (approximately $150 million today) and be worshipped in the bargain!

Of more worth is ONE honest man to society, than all the bullies who wear the crown of a king!

The Main Points of Chapter Two

☐ Paine says that many of the differences that occur between people happen naturally. For example, some people become rich, some become poor. Some can be weaker and become exploited, while others can become greedy.

☐ But if humankind entered this world as equals, how is it there are privileged people who remain privileged from generation to generation? How did kings rise above everyone else? Why does governing power continue from father to son (hereditary succession)? How did this happen?

☐ Paine argues that hereditary succession did not happen naturally, but rose from wrongdoings. Furthermore, having allowed power to remain in a monarchy has produced many wars, countless deaths, and immeasurable other evils.

Chapter 3

Thoughts on the Present State of America

In the past, changing from a British colonist to an American was just an idea by some. Citizens of the colonies felt they were British and loyal subjects of the King. Today, I offer simple facts, truthful arguments and common sense, and ask that you put aside all fears or feelings you presently have, look beyond today, and just listen to me for a short time.

An **enormous** amount of information has been written about the struggle between England and America. Men from all walks of life have involved themselves in this argument. They have unsuccessfully argued, or tried to persuade, all others of their ideas.

The debate is now over! No more Kings! Weapons must decide this contest. The king ignored our pleas and has attacked us several times!

This is the greatest cause ever! This is not the fight for righteousness of a town, a city, a **province** or a kingdom, but a fight for a continent which contains at least 1/8th of the **habitable** globe. This is not a cause for a day, a year, or an age, but forever. The future generations are now involved, and will be affected to the end of time.

> **Province**: a territory that has been around a long time and has history.

The events going on right now are the seeds of a **unification** of faith and honor of all thirteen colonies on our continent. The smallest fracture between us now will be like a tiny carving into a small oak sapling, which will grow large over time, and future generations will be able to read our failure in giant letters.

> **Habitable**: an area of the world that where people can live.

> **Unification**: to bring together.

No more arguing. We must go to arms! A new plan and new thinking is forming.

Anything that was planned or proposed prior to the 19th of April (Lexington & Concord) is old news. Maybe they were good ideas at the time, but the **hostilities** have changed that. When we tried to mend our disagreements fairly, Britain reacted with force, which has failed. And we offered friendship, *which we now withdraw!*

*   *   *

Quotes from History:

"An injured friend is the bitterest of foes."
— Thomas Jefferson

Continental . . . *Continental* . . . **Continental**

Have you noticed that lots of things were called "Continental?" For example,

- **Continental Congress**
- **Continental Army**
- **Paine talked of being "Continental"**

As the idea of independence grew, the colonies were trying to negotiate with one voice: one continent. Although the 13 colonies were separate provinces, the unity of those provinces would create the real power for change.

To be fair, let us look at the advantages and disadvantages of our connection and dependence on Great Britain.

I. Some have said that America has **prospered** under Great Britain, and we must keep this connection for future happiness. This is absolutely false!

> **Prospered:** to achieve economic success

Things change over time. If this was not true would infants who first just fed on milk never need meat? When we are born, are our first twenty years of life going to be exactly like our next twenty years? I say that America would have prospered as much, and probably more, if no European power had controlled her. These colonies have had rich success with the goods we sell to markets in Europe . . . and will continue to do so.

II. Others say Great Britain has protected us. Yes, she has defended this continent (French & Indian War), even though she would have defended almost anyone for profits and power.

reat Britain's interest in us has always been for money, not affection. She did not protect the colonies from our enemies but her enemies. In fact, she fights with countries we do not have quarrel with, but who remain our enemies because of our connection to Great Britain. If we separate, we will immediately be at peace with France and Spain.

> **III**. Parliament has said that all of the thirteen colonies have no relationship with one another, except by way of Britain as the parent. For example, the only reason that Pennsylvania and New Jersey are sister colonies is because they are both linked to England. But, when England is at war with Spain and France, suddenly the King believes we are all related as one, to help in those wars against Spain or France.

f Great Britain is our parent, then shame on her. Even **brutes** don't devour their young, or savages make war on their own families! The phrase "parent" or "mother country" was invented by the King and his **parasites** to take advantage of our trust and loyalty.

Parasite: an organism living off another and giving nothing of value in return.

urope, not England, is the parent country of America. For many, many years, people seeking civil and religious liberty have left every part of Europe, and have come to our continent to find **sanctuary**. They have fled not from a loving mother country, but the cruelty of a monster. Years ago, England's tyranny chased the first settlers to this land, and England continues to chase their **descendants** today.

Sanctuary: a place of safety and protection.

Descendants: children, offspring, or close relatives.

First of all, it is selfish of England to even say they are the parent of us all because not one-third of the colonies' inhabitants are of English descent!

Our friendships continue to grow with almost every European country as we generously accept all who want to move here. Whether they come from England, Holland, Germany or Sweden, we come together as Americans. We don't make the distinction of being English or Dutch or Germans, we think as one continent and one people.'

> **Farcical:** laughable, absurd, ludicrous.

Is it our duty is to reconcile with England? **Farcical**! The first king of England, William the Conqueror, was a Frenchman, and half the peers of England are descendants from the same country. So by the same flawed reasoning, England should be ruled by France.

Much has been said of the combined strength of Britain and her American colonies. That together, we are stronger than all others. But, the people of our colonies do not have a quarrel with the world; they do not support Britain's wars in Asia, Africa, or Europe. Our plan is **commerce**.

> **Commerce:** buying and selling goods on a large scale, using ocean-going ships to transport the goods.

We will remain safe without Britain. All of Europe benefits from having America as a free port. Plus, we have little gold or silver to attract invaders.

I challenge the biggest fan of reconciliation to show a single advantage this continent will gain by being connected with Great Britain. No advantage is gained! We continue to sell our corn in any market in Europe, and we will always be welcome to buy the goods of other countries at will.

By breaking our connection with Great Britain we solve many difficulties. We have a duty to mankind to end our relationship, because we are pulled into European wars and conflicts with nations who are, or would be, our friends. Because Europe is our market for trade, we should not partner with any one country.

Europe is too thickly planted with Kingdoms, and whenever war breaks out between England and another Kingdom, our trade goes to ruin *because of our connection to Great Britain*!

> ***Everything that is right or natural pleads for separation.***
> ***The blood of the slain,***
> ***the weeping voice of nature cries,***
> ***'tis time to part.***

Even the distance, which the Almighty put between England and America, is proof that the authority of one over the other was never the intention of heaven.

How this continent was discovered, and the way it was settled, adds even more evidence. The **Reformation** happened before the discovery of America, as if the Almighty meant to open a sanctuary for victimized people who were never offered friendship or safety in their birth country. They found their safety here.

> **Reformation, The:** In Europe around 1517, religious life and how people participated in faith began to change. Many people began to reject the main religion of the time. Decades later, people seeking religious freedom found their way to the shores of North America.

*   *   *

Britain's authority over this continent must end. Our present constitution is not built to last, and certainly not strong enough to hand over to our future generations. We need to do the work of separation

now; otherwise we are jeopardizing the next generation shamefully, and running them into debt.

I try not to insult, but the people who believe in **reconciliation** fall into one of the following categories:

Reconciliation: to patch-up a friendship or give up something to end a disagreement.

I. Interested men, who personally profit from this relationship and are not to be trusted

II. Weak men . . . who cannot see

III. Prejudiced men . . . who will not see

and

Quotes from History:

"One today is worth two tomorrows."
— **Ben Franklin**

IV. A certain group of unemotional men who think the European world is a fine place, much better than it actually is.

And it is the last group of people (#4), who believe wrongly and will cause more disasters to this continent than all the other three.

Many colonists live far from the everyday scenes of **sorrow** that are happening everyday. The evil does not always travel the distance to their doors for them to personally witness how un-secure and at-risk their property in America really is.

For you to understand, please let our imaginations carry us a few moments to Boston, where you will witness firsthand the reasons to reject a power we cannot trust.

Those colonists who live in Boston, who just a few months ago were happy and secure, are now trapped and starving, or must come out of the city to beg. If they leave, they will be robbed of everything they own by the British Soldiers stationed there. They have become prisoners in their own city, and face real harm if the **Continental Army** attacks the city to save them; for they will be caught in the middle of the fury of both armies.

Some, with **passive** natures, who still hope for the best are quick to call out, "come, come we shall be friends again for all this," but can you love, honor, and serve the power that has brought fire and sword into your land?

f you feel you can still excuse or forgive the wrongs of England then I ask you this . . .

* Has *your* house been burned down?

* Has *your* property been destroyed as you watched?

* Have *your* wife and children been sleeping on no bed, and going hungry?!

* Have *you* lost a parent or child and been left poor and sobbing?

If *you* have not experienced any of these, then do not judge those who have.

f you have experienced any of those horrors and you can still forgive and shake hands with the murderers, *then you are unworthy of being a husband, father, friend, lover, or whatever you do in life, for you have the heart of a coward*!

t is disgusting to even consider that this continent remain under an outside power. I am not exaggerating... it is important to examine these events with real human emotions. I do not tell you of the horrors that have taken place to encourage revenge but to urge you to take action before it is too late. If we act now, having these winter months to prepare is invaluable.

ll our reasonable attempts for peace have not worked. Our prayers to the King have been rejected with **contempt**, and have proven that we just flatter arrogant kings and make them more absolute with our repeated **petitions**.

> **Contempt:** A complete disrespect or lack of respect; disobedience.

> **Petitions:** Formal written requests or complaints, usually asking for change.

$\mathcal{S}$o, since only blows will do, for God's sake… let us finally separate so we don't let our next generation inherit this violent fight.

$\mathcal{T}$o say they will never again try and pass restrictive laws without our permission is just poor guessing and laziness. We thought they wouldn't try again after the repeal of the Stamp Act, and look what happened two years later! (See 1767 on time line.)

$\mathcal{B}$ritain's government cannot fairly manage this continent. There is too much happening here. A power so far from us, and ignorant of us, does not have the skill to manage the many details. If they cannot conquer us, they cannot govern us. Our requests now must travel three or four thousand miles, and then we wait four or five months for an answer. When we finally get the answer, it takes another five or six months for the explanation! To continue in this manner will be looked upon as folly and childishness in a few short years. There was a time when this type of governing was appropriate, and there is now an appropriate time for it to stop.

$\mathcal{S}$mall islands…that cannot defend themselves are the proper places for Kingdoms to govern, but it is crazy for an entire continent to be forever governed by an island. The moon is not bigger than the earth! America is large; Britain is small, and to be controlled by Britain reverses the order of nature; it is obvious the two belong to different systems. England belongs to Europe—America belongs to itself.

*   *   *

Quotes from History:

"Lost time is never found again."

— Ben Franklin

---

have no selfish motives for separation and independence; I am positive it is in our continent's true interest to do it.

ince Britain has not shown the slightest interest in **compromise** and reasonable terms for **allegiance**, the goal we seek must be worth the price we have already paid in blood and money. We do not just want to have **Minister North**, or his detestable **Junto**, removed . . . that would not be worth our struggle. If we are forced to take up guns, if every one of us must become a soldier, we need to permanently remove the control of the King over us.

Allegiance: Loyalty

Junto: A group of persons joined for a common purpose. (A variation of Junta.)

t would be a great stupidity to pay a "Bunker Hill" price for short term success.

We must not go unrewarded for the sacrifices we have made since the breaking out of hostilities. Otherwise, it would be like spending the entire value of your house on a lawsuit against someone who just **trespasses** on your grass. We must receive fair value!

I was a big fan of reconciliation BEFORE the deadly April 19th, 1775, but once that tragedy happened, I rejected the hard-hearted King of England forever. He says he is the "father of the people" while he heartlessly hears of their slaughter, and sleeps peacefully knowing that the blood of those killed is his fault.

*   *   *

Let us suppose we make up. What would be the result? The RUIN of our continent I answer, and for several reasons:

First, the King will still be in power, and he has shown that he is an enemy of **liberty**. He thirsts for total unchecked power. Is there anyone here in America who is so ignorant not to believe that the King will make all the laws, and then, only laws that will suit his purpose? Is there any doubt that the whole power of the Crown will be used to keep us down?

We are already greater than the King wishes us to be. Should the person who is jealous of us, and jealous of our success, be the person to govern us?

It is ridiculous that a king who could even be 21 years of age, which has happened a lot, can say to millions of older and wiser people, than himself, that certain laws should be allowed and others **banned**. And, the King lives in England – not here! He will always act first for England's defense, but never act as strongly for us. It would always be in England's best interest for us to be in second place behind "her." Men don't just change from enemies to friends after just changing names.

I believe the King would **repeal** all the acts we want cancelled, get rid of all the taxes we are complaining about, and do whatever we want, so he

could regain power over us again. Then he will start a new plan, little by little, so we hardly notice, that will slowly accomplish later what he couldn't do now by force.

So, reconciliation and destruction are almost the same thing!

Repeal: To stop or reverse something, often a law or new tax, through legislative power.

Second, even if the King gave us the best terms, they would only be temporary. And then, during those times, people would be nervous and untrusting; things would be strict and uneven. **Emigrants** with money would choose not to come

Emigrant: People who leave their country to move to another.

to a country that has a government always on the edge of disorder, and others who live here now…will leave!

The best argument is… independence and one government. It is the only solution that can keep the peace of this continent and avoid civil wars.

Thousands of people have already been ruined by British **barbarity**. Those who have sacrificed have done it for our Liberty! They cannot go back. They have nothing left to lose, and scorn surrender. Besides, everyone in the colonies no longer feels close to the British government. They feel more like a teenager preparing to leave home.

In 1775, women were rarely recognized directly in the events of the day. It was common for writings to refer to people only in the masculine. Countries, however, as they are today, were usually referred to in the feminine.

Paine argued that unless the colonists declared independence soon, America would be too unstable a place to attract new citizens.

government which cannot preserve the peace is no government at all – so we waste our money! There is so much to fear in a patched up relationship with England instead of independence.

here is now such a spirit of goodwill among all the colonies for our own continental government, every reasonable

Barbarity: Acts of cruelty

person can be easy and happy. Only childish people would fear that the colonies would try to dominate each other if England wasn't controlling us. The colonies are perfect equals, and being equal creates no jealousy.

*   *   *

The true fear of Independence is that there is no design on how to do it yet. So I offer some suggestions for a plan.

Let our own **assemblies** be voted in yearly and have a president who gets his authority from the Continental Congress.

> **Assemblies:** A group of people who gather to discuss and create laws.

Let the colonies be divided into districts with representatives going to Congress. Each district can send 30 representatives, totaling 390. (13 X 30 = 390.) Representatives from Congress will choose the first President for a one-year term. The following year, the next Congress will get to elect the next President from the other twelve colonies, and so on, till all colonies have had a President elected from their district. Any new laws brought forth will need to be approved by at least 3/5ths of the Congress (a minimum of 234 representatives).

Next, the Continental Government's job is to secure the freedom and property of all men and allow the free exercise of any religion. This new government will provide the greatest amount of happiness for the least amount of cost.

In absolute governments, the king is law.
In America, the law is the king.

*   *   *

Having our own government is our natural right, and it makes more sense for us to create our own constitution now, while we have the time and desire, and can be done sensibly.

Those of you who oppose independence do not realize what you are doing! You are opening a door to never-ending tyranny! Colonists by the thousands think it is glorious to push out the barbarous and hellish power from our continent which has stirred up the Indians and Africans on these shores to destroy us. This cruelty has double guilt…it brutalizes us and is treacherous to them! To talk of friendship is madness. There is little hope that our affection for one another will increase as the years go by, when we will have ten times more worries to argue over.

Those of you who talk to us of harmony and reconciliation, can you go back in time? You cannot reunite Britain and America. The last thread is now broken. The people of England are talking against us. There are injuries that cannot be forgiven.

Mr. Straham,

You are a Member of Parliament and one of that majority which has doomed my country to destruction. You have begun to burn our towns and murder our people. Look upon your hands! They are stained with the blood of your relations! You and I were long friends. You are now my enemy, and I am yours.

Ben Franklin

Even Benjamin Franklin believed there were injuries that could not be forgiven when he wrote this letter:

The Almighty has given us this **inextinguishable** want of Liberty for a good and wise purpose!

O! Ye that love mankind!

Ye who dare oppose not only tyranny but the tyrant, stand forth!

Inextinguishable:
Unquenchable, something that cannot be put out or stopped.

Freedom has been chased away around the globe.

Asia and Africa expelled her.

Europe regards her like a stranger.

England has given her warning to leave.

O! let us receive freedom and prepare an asylum for mankind!

The king's dignity still requires full
and absolute submission.

— Peer

Main Points of Chapter Three

☐ In chapter three, Paine tries to convince the colonists that it is ridiculous for an island to govern a continent. Especially an island that is 3000 miles away. Not only that, but the present government treats its American Colonies cruelly, is hurting commerce between the colonies and the rest of the world, and has every intention of restricting the freedoms of America even further through more taxes and direct rule. Moreover, the recent violence has shown that the king really does not care for the citizens of America, and he does not deserve their loyalty anymore.

☐ Opportunities for great change occur rarely, and Paine wants to convince the colonists that the present time is perfect to declare independence. Otherwise, the opportunity is lost forever.

Chapter 4

The Present Ability of America, With Some Miscellaneous Thoughts

I have never met anyone in England or America who did not believe that a separation between the two countries would eventually take place. But we seem to lack the judgment on when the right time for this independence is to happen. Let's take a survey of things in hopes of finding this right time. But, we don't need to look long because the time has found us!

Our great strength lies in the unity of our thirteen colonies, not the number of citizens we have. However, we have enough citizens to **repel** the force of the entire world. At this time, our continent has the largest body of armed and **disciplined** men of any nation under heaven.

Our united colonies have enough people for a sufficient army. We don't have a Navy, but Britain would never let us have one, so we'd be no better off in the future than we are now. But if we wait, the timber within our reach will get used up, and then getting more to build ships will be difficult.

$\mathcal{B}$ecause of our current decrease in trade (Boston Harbor is closed) we have a sufficient number of citizens and jobs for them to do. Lack of trade creates our army, and the needs of an army will create new trade.

$\mathcal{I}$f we can leave future generations with an established form of government and an independent constitution, its value would be great at any price. But to spend millions on just getting the king to repeal a few **vile** acts is too expensive at any cost, and would be piling cruelty and debt upon our future generations by leaving them the great work WE should do now! Honorable men would not do that, but those with narrow hearts would.

> **Vile**: disgustingly bad, morally wicked.

> **Boatswain**: a naval officer in charge of maintaining the hull (body) of a ship.

* * *

$\mathcal{B}$ritain is weighted down with debt of almost one-hundred-forty-million sterling (approximately $20,000,000,000 in today's money). Much of this debt was used to create a large navy. Americans have no debt...but no navy. However, we could spend 1/20th of England's national debt and build a navy just as large. Because, right now, the navy of England is not worth more than 3 ½ million pounds sterling. I will show you.

$\mathcal{T}$he cost of building the following ships with masts, yards, sails, and rigging, together with eight months of labor costs for **boatswains** and carpenters, and finally **sea stores**, as calculated by Mr. Burchett, Secretary to the British Navy:

Cost of Ships		
For a ship of:	*100 guns*	*35,553 pounds sterling*
	90	29,886
	80	23,638
	70	17,785
	60	14,197
	50	10,606
	40	7,558
	30	5,846
	20	3,710

*E*ngland was at its most glorious in 1757, and she had a total of 251 warships in various sizes. The combined value of those ships was £3,500,000 Pounds Sterling (the British monetary unit):

Value of British Navy			
Ships	*Guns*	*Cost of One*	*Cost of All*
6	100	35,553	213,318
12	90	29,886	358,632
12	80	23,638	283,656
43	70	17,785	764,755
35	60	14,197	496,895
40	50	10,606	424,240

Value of British Navy (continued)			
Ships	*Guns*	*Cost of One*	*Cost of All*
45	40	7,558	340,110
58	20	3,710	215,180
	85 misc.	2,000	170,000
		COST	3,266,786
		Remains for Guns	233,214
		Value of British Navy	3,500,000 pounds sterling

*S*o, while England is buried under considerable debt, we can create an equal Navy for much less cost, and carry a much smaller debt. Besides, having a national debt, a debt we all carry together, is a very honorable thing.

*A*merica is extremely capable of building a **fleet** of ships. We produce tar, timber, iron and rope all right here on our shores. We don't need to **import** anything to build a Navy.

Fleet: A number of warships under a single or unified command.

*M*aking ships should become our most important task. It is the best money we could spend. A newly built Navy is worth more than its cost. And then, our ships will be joined into one because they will be able to trade and to protect!

Import: To bring items into your country produced in or shipped from another country.

*L*et's build them. If we don't want them, we will sell them for a lot of gold and silver. What better time to build than now?—with the British having closed Boston Harbor we have many unemployed sailors and **shipwrights**, and our forests are full of good timber.

*W*e used to build ships of war in New England forty years ago, why not now? Ship building is America's greatest pride, and we would soon build warships better than the rest of the world. Because of our extremely long coastline, we are the only country blessed with great supplies of wood.

*S*ixty years ago, we could keep our doors unlocked, but not today. We need improved methods of defense to match our increased prosperity. We need a navy to protect us from England and pirates as well.

Spanish "Piece of Eight," or "Pillar Dollars," common money in Colonial America.

In the 18th century there were no paychecks or automated bank transfers. Ships carrying "treasure chests" of coins and bullion (bars of gold and silver) served as floating "banks" for an army serving somewhere overseas. If a ship sank, many soldiers would not receive their pay for a long, long time.

ome might say, if we make up with England, she will protect us, but I ask how?! A navy that is three or four thousand miles away is of little use. We must protect ourselves!

he English have many fearsome ships, but not even a tenth of them are in shape and ready to go at any one time. Many of their ships don't even exist anymore, but their names are still on a list to scare the enemy into thinking they have more ships than they do.

oreover, the English navy is needed and spread out all over the world! We do not need to fear fighting all the ships in their entire navy. Probably very few. We will have the advantage because we will be fighting on our own shores, and they will need to sail three to four thousand miles to attack us. Afterward, they must sail back and forth long distances for repairs, supplies and new sailors.

Hemp: A tough fibrous plant used to make a strong rope.

n almost all the important areas we have great amounts. **Hemp** grows in great quantity, so rope for ship **rigging** is plentiful. We make the best iron in the world. We can make cannon at anytime. We already produce **saltpeter** and gunpowder every day. Our knowledge improves by the hour.

Rigging: Ropes and chains to work sails and other moveable parts of a ship.

e have always had courage, so why do we **hesitate**? From Britain we can expect nothing but ruin. If we allow them to govern America again, this

Saltpeter: A mineral that, when mixed with sulphur and charcoal, makes gunpowder.

continent will not be worth living in! Jealousies will always be erupting. We have large amounts of land not yet settled, why let the king give it to his worthless friends and family? We can use this land for ourselves.

There is risk in waiting. History has shown us that as economies get larger, people get too busy making a living to do anything else.

The more men have to lose, the less they are willing to take risk. The rich, are in general, slaves to fear.

Youth is the seed-time of good habits, in nations and in individuals. Right now, our thirteen colonies need one another. But if we wait another fifty years, it would become colony against colony, each probably stronger, but acting individually and rejecting the other's assistance. Wise men in the future will grieve that a union had not been formed before. The bonds and friendships we will form in our country's

Quotes from History

"All tyranny needs to gain a foothold is for people of good conscience to remain silent." — Thomas Jefferson early years will be the strongest and longest lasting. We are young, we have **withstood** our troubles, and our future generations will be glorious.

et us learn from the mistakes of other nations. Chances like this happen only once! Others let their opportunity slip away and were conquered by others who forced their laws upon them. When William the Conqueror subdued England, he gave them law at the point of a sword. *We can form our own government now!*

*   *   *

Quotes from History

America is a mere bully, from one end to the other, and Bostonians by far the greatest bullies.

— General Thomas Gage

---

everal pages ago, I had some thoughts on organizing our government (Continental Charter), a bond between us all to support the rights of all people, of all religions, and protect individual personal property and personal freedoms. Treating others fairly makes long friends.

bout religion, I believe all governments have the duty to protect believers of all faiths.

If men can put aside their selfish belief,
their veiled soul, and self-centered principles,
the cause of those fears will disappear.
Suspicion is the friend of mean souls,
and the curse of all good society.

I also mentioned the necessity of a large and equal representation, and this is most important! A small number of voters, or a small number of representatives, is dangerous! For our future generations we need to remember that virtue is not inherited.

*   *   *

To conclude, there are many excellent reasons to quickly announce an open and unwavering declaration for independence:

> **Mediate:** Get two or more quarreling people or organizations together in order to bring about an agreement.

*1*st. We need to break from England and go to war so that another country can **mediate** our differences.

*2*nd. It would be dishonorable to accept help from France and Spain, and then just compromise or mend our differences with England. If we stay with Britain, even after France and Spain have helped us, not only would Britain remain the enemy of those two countries, but we would again have to become the enemy of France and Spain as well. These would be terrible consequences for those who offered to be our friend and tried to help us gain American independence.

*3*rd. While we are still connected to Britain, we are considered to be Rebels (outlaws). And the idea of armed outlaws in any country scares governments.

*4*th. If we publish a paper and send it to all other countries explaining all the miseries we have suffered, all the peaceful methods we have tried, explaining why we cannot live happily or safely under the evil British government, and at the same time pledging to these other nations of our peace towards them and our wish to enter into trade with them, this paper would produce more good results for us than a boatload of petitions to Britain.

Until we declare independence, we cannot stand with other nations.

Taking these steps may, at first, appear strange and difficult, but with time will become familiar and rewarding. And until we declare independence, our entire continent will feel like a man who continues putting off some unpleasant business day after day, yet knows it must be done, hates to begin it, wishes it were over, and is continuously haunted with the thoughts of its necessity.

We have it in our power to begin the world over again.

* * *

Main Points of Chapter Four

☐ Paine wants to convince the colonists they can win a war for independence. Although Britain has the strongest army in the world, Paine argues that England has a unique series of challenges. For example, much of the British Navy is spread out all across the globe, so only a small percentage of ships can be used to bring over troops and supplies. In addition, fighting a war 3000 miles from home would be extremely difficult for the king to manage. Furthermore, America is rich in resources and manpower.

☐ Next, America really does not have a quarrel with other countries like Britain does. Declaring independence would immediately mend relationships with the rest of the world which would result in greater commerce. Without a declaration of independence, there is great risk that the rest of the world would only view America as an extremely unstable place.

In 1787, Thomas Paine traveled back to Europe, and eventually to his native land of England, where he tried to convince English citizens to dump King George III. Paine's Enemies issues these "coins," or Conder Tokens entitled "End of Pain[e]" to warn British citizens that a rebellion in England could mirror the disasters of the French Revolution—where King Louis XVI was beheaded and Napoleon took over control of the country and its people.

SECTION II

Commerce in the Colonies

"For no nation in a state of foreign dependence, limited in its commerce, and cramped and fettered in its legislative powers, can ever arrive at any material eminence."

— Thomas Paine

Chapter 5
Coins in the Colonies

*C*oins, as well as paper money, played a major role in the development of the Colonies. Without a form of money, it would have been very difficult and probably impossible to develop a vibrant economy.

Silver shilling from Great Britain. The king's face was on most of the coinage and brought to the colonies in small amounts.

Great Britain included Ireland. Above is an Irish half-penny with King George's portrait on the obverse, and an Irish harp, the symbol of Ireland, on the reverse. (Below) A common coin: the English half penny.

Farthings (left) circulated throughout the colonies. They also bore the king's portrait, but were about one-half the size of a half-pence. Two farthings equaled only a half-penny!

Here are three unidentified coins. How might you identify them?

Virginia's charter allowed it to coin money, but it never did until 1773. This was the only coin authorized to be minted by the colonies. However, by this time, there was so much civil unrest, the coins were delayed and only circulated for a short time. A bust

of King George III appears on the face of the coin; the back is imprinted with the shield of the colony of Virginia, bearing the Arms of the King.

*   *   *

1775 Calendar Coin
(next page)

Calendar medals were popular between 1752 and 1860 in England and the American Colonies. Eventually, paper calendars became cheaper and easier to produce. This calendar medal, about the size of a silver dollar, was coined in Birmingham England in 1775.

Note: major observance days included:

❏   The King's birthday;

❏   Queen's birthday;

❏   The Prince of Wales' (king's first son and heir apparent) birthday.

This remarkable coin also showed phases of the moon and many religious observances.

(Why do you think that Independence Day, July 4th, is not on the coin?)

Chapter 6
Mercantilism and Why the Colonists Needed Pocket Change!

✓ Read "Coins of the Colonies" (pages 61-64)

✓ Review Timeline 1764 (page 4)

Great Britain never let the colonies produce their own coins (and they wouldn't let them print their own currency either). England would send over just an inadequate number of copper coins (mostly with the face of the king on the front) for the colonists to use. Furthermore, it was illegal to send gold or silver coins to the colonies.
  Why?

In the 1700's, many governments believed their nation's wealth and power had a lot to do with how much gold they could get. Remember, there is only so much gold in the world (in other words, gold is a **finite** metal).

> **Finite**: A limited number or quantity of something. Then it is gone.

The colonies were sometimes restricted on what they could make. Also, many of the items that the colonies did produce could only be shipped to England. If the colonies were allowed to coin their own money, Britain was afraid they would spend that money in a lot of other countries. So, with very few coins, many colonial businesses found it a lot easier to trade mostly with the "Mother Country" using credit, IOUs,

and barter. (Now would be a good time to look at February 1775 on the timeline again too.)

England would then take many of those goods, purchased from the colonies, and sell them to the other countries for more of that precious gold.

(Remember when Boston Harbor was closed? Businesses in the American Colonies and in Great Britain couldn't collect the money that was owed to them. People on both sides of the Atlantic suffered.)

However, the American Colonists were very creative. They used coins from all over the world to try and solve their "pocket change problem." It was common to have a pocket full of coins from Spain, Holland, France, Portugal, and other countries. Since the values of coins were different in every country (depending on what they were made of and how heavy they were) you had to be pretty good at math to calculate what something might cost.

Counterfeiting was also very popular in the American colonies just as it was popular in Great Britain. Why? Because the colonists needed pocket change.

> **Counterfeiting**: To make illegal copies of something. Counterfeit coins usually had less valuable metal.

Chapter 7
What's the Deal with
Early American Printing?

*I*f you have not yet discovered it, English writing from 18th Century occasionally looks like a foreign language. But, how can this be? English is . . . English, right?

Well, yes . . . and no.

It was common practice a couple hundred years ago to write certain words a certain way that is very different than what we see and write today. For example, if a word had a double "s" (for example, the word "possible"), it was common to write the double "ss" as double "ff." So, the word "possible" would be written "poffible"—two fs instead of a pair of s's

It is also important to note that a single "s" could have been written like an "f." Or, in the middle of the word, the "s" could look like an "f" but at the end of the word it was written as "s."

Confused? You are not alone. If you are not careful, you can really confuse the meanings of some words. This practice continued until the 20th century.

Below is an example (on the left) of writing from the Colonial era, with how it should be read (on the right) today.

Original (1776)	How it Reads Now

COMMON SENSE.   29

Nation and fet it together by the ears. A   . . . set . . .
pretty bufinefs indeed for a man to be al-   . . . business . . .
lowed eight hundred thoufand flerling a year   . . . thousand sterling . . .
for, and worfhipped into the bargain! Of   . . . worshipped . . .
more worth is one honeft man to fociety   . . . honest . . .
and in the fight of God, than all the crown-   . . . sight . . .
ed Ruffians that ever lived.

THOUGHTS, on the prefent STATE of   *Can you find the words in the original version?*
AMERICAN AFFAIRS.

IN the following pages I offer nothing more
than fimple facts, plain arguments, and
common fenfe: and have no other preliminaries to fettle with the Reader, than that
he will diveft himfelf of prejudice and pre-
poffeffion, and fuffer his reafon and his
feelings to determine for themfelves: that
he will put *on* or rather that he will not put
off the true character of a man, and gene-
roufly enlarge his views beyond the prefent
day.

Volumes have been written on the fubject
of the ftruggle between England and America. Men of all ranks have embarked in
the controverfy, from different motives,
and with various defigns; but all have been
ineffectual,

SECTION III

Parchment in the Colonies:
A War of Thought, Words, and Actions

John Marlin Will's "The Bostonians in Distress."

Chapter 8
The Quartering Act

The Quartering Act, passed by the British Parliament in 1765, assured that His Majesty's Regular Troops and the colonists would be seeing a lot more of each other. The colonies welcomed the troops during the French and Indian War (known in Europe as the Seven Years' War), but were very intimidated by having a standing army stationed in their midst after that war ended.

Benjamin Franklin wrote in his *Poor Richard's Almanac*, "Fish and visitors stink after three days." The near future would prove the wisdom of Franklin's words.

* * *

✓ Review 1766 and 1770 on the timeline.

✓ Review these paragraphs from page 36.

From the adaptation of *Common Sense:*

"For you to understand, please let our imaginations carry us a few moments to Boston, where you will witness firsthand the reasons to reject a power we cannot trust.

Those colonists who live in Boston, who just a few months ago were happy and secure, are now trapped and starving, or must come out of the city to beg. If they leave, they will be robbed of everything they own by the British Soldiers stationed there. They have become prisoners in their own city, and face real harm if the Continental Army attacks the city to save them; for they will be caught in the middle of the fury of both armies."

(About the Quartering Act): Armies don't do much good if they sit around all day, so British Regular Troops would spend much of their time marching from one place to another.

The soldiers were far from home, paid little, and generally hated by colonists who resented they were there; so desertion was a problem. The Quartering Act was actually several laws deciding where the soldiers could sleep, and what would happen to soldiers if they deserted. There were buildings (barracks) set aside for use by the troops, but if there were not enough buildings; the act could be interpreted to have private homes made available for the soldiers to "quarter" in.

From original Quartering Act: *" . . . after all such 'publick houses' were filled. . . . to take, hire and make fit for the reception of his Majesty's forces, such and so many uninhabited houses, outhouses, barns, or other buildings as shall be necessary."*

*   *   *

The end result: His Majesty's Army pitched tents throughout the city of Boston. The soldiers, living next to angry Patriots, were soon involved in street brawls and eventually the "Boston Massacre" in 1770.

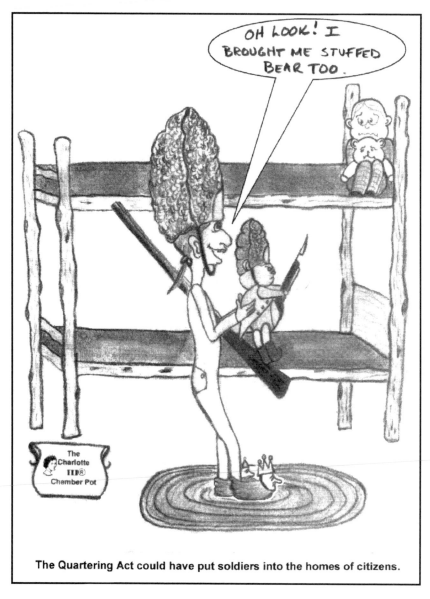

The Quartering Act could have put soldiers into the homes of citizens.

British soldiers remained in Boston until 1776, when General George Washington forced them out with the Continental Army.

Chapter 9

The Boston Port Act

(Adapted Text)

☞ Review Situation Map (page 2)

The Boston Port Act was one of the "Coercive Acts," (see March 1774 on Timeline). The Colonists called them the "Intolerable Acts." Closing Boston Harbor was in reaction to a little party the colonists had during December of 1774.

Why wouldn't England be thrilled about a party?

* * *

The Boston Port Act (adapted)

British Parliament: 1774

An act to shut down the delivery or shipping of goods, wares, and merchandise, within the town and harbor of Boston, in the province of Massachusetts Bay, North America.

WHEREAS dangerous uprisings have occurred in the town of Boston, Massachusetts Bay New England, by various misguided persons who have tried to subvert his Majesty's government and destroy the public peace of the town. During these insurrections, certain valuable cargoes of teas, being the property of the East India Company, on board certain ships lying within harbor of Boston, were seized and destroyed.

In the present condition of the town and harbor, the business of his Majesty's subjects cannot be conducted safely, or the taxes payable to his Majesty be collected.

Therefore, the Majesty's Customs Officers shall be immediately removed from the said town; and by decision of the King, the House of Lords, and the Commons of this Parliament, that starting June 1st 1774 there will be no loading or unloading of ships within the town of Boston, or on any shore in the Harbor of Boston, between **Nahant Point** on the eastern side of the bay entrance, and **Alderton Point** on the western side of the bay entrance. And in between those two points; no island, creek, landing place, bank, or other place within the bay, into any ship or boat, any goods, wares, or merchandise whatsoever, to *be shipped* to any other country, province or place whatsoever. Any attempt to do so will result in the loss of the ships and all goods.

If any wharf owner, wharf manager, employees or servants knowingly attempt *to bring* in any goods, they will be fined triple the value of such merchandise, and all items used; ships, horses, carriages, boats, etc. will be seized as well.

If any ship is found anchored or seen hovering within one league (about 3 miles) from the said bay, it shall be lawful for any admiral, chief commander, or commissioned officer of his Majesty's fleet or ships of war, to force that vessel to depart within six hours. Otherwise, that ship may be fired upon, boarded, and taken.

*T*he Majesty's ships are exempt from this act. Furthermore, ships carrying food or fuel for the inhabitants of Boston from neighboring colonies will be allowed after being searched and given a cocket (certified document). In addition, ships already doing business in the harbor have 14 days to leave.

*A*ll seizures and penalties collected by this act shall be prosecuted by any admiral, chief commander, commissioned officer, or Majesty's customs officer. If any of these authorized individuals are found taking a bribe to allow the loading or unloading of any goods, they will be fined the sum of 500 pounds for every offense. And for any individual offering a bribe to an authorized official, they will be fined the sum of 50 pounds.

*A*ny contract that existed before June 1st 1774 for the loading or unloading of goods is automatically cancelled.

*W*hen the Majesty and his Privy Council have been convinced that order has been restored in Boston, and that the trade of Great Britain can be conducted safely and taxes collected—his Majesty shall appoint as many customs officials as he sees fit, and reopen the harbor. However, before the harbor can be reopened, the inhabitants of Boston must make full restitution for the cargoes of tea destroyed during the riots and insurrections in the months of November and December 1773, and in the month of January 1774.

*　*　*

The Boston Port Act (Original Text)

British Parliament - 1774

An act to discontinue, in such manner, and for such time as are therein mentioned, the landing and discharging, lading or shipping, of goods, wares, and merchandise, at the town, and within the harbour, of Boston, in the province of Massachuset's Bay, in North America.

WHEREAS dangerous commotions and insurrections have been fomented and raised in the town of Boston, in the province of Massachuset's Bay, in New England, by divers ill-affected persons, to the subversion of his Majesty's government, and to the utter destruction of the publick peace, and good order of the said town; in which commotions and insurrections certain valuable cargoes of teas, being the property of the East India Company, and on board certain vessels lying within the bay or harbour of Boston, were seized and destroyed: And whereas, in the present condition of the said town and harbour, the commerce of his Majesty's subjects cannot be safely carried on there, nor the customs payable to his Majesty duly collected; and it is therefore expedient that the officers of his Majesty's customs should be forthwith removed from the said town: May it please your Majesty that it may be enacted; and be it enacted by the King's most excellent majesty, by and with the advice and consent of the lords spiritual and temporal, and commons, in this present parliament assembled, and by the authority of the same, That from and after the first day of June, one thousand seven hundred and seventy-four, it shall not be lawful for any person or persons whatsoever to lade put, or cause or procure to be laden or put, off or from any quay, wharf, or other place, within the said town of Boston, or in or upon any part of the shore of the bay, commonly called The Harbour of

Boston, between a certain headland or point called Nahant Point, on the eastern side of the entrance into the said bay, and a certain other headland or point called Alderton Point, on the western side of the entrance into the said bay, or in or upon any island, creek, landing place, bank, or other place, within the said bay or headlands, into any ship, vessel, lighter, boat, or bottom, any goods, wares, or merchandise whatsoever, to be transported or carried into any other country, province or place whatsoever, or into any other part of the said province of the Massachuset's Bay, in New England; or to take up, discharge, or lay on land, or cause or procure to be taken up, discharged, or laid on land, within the said town, or in or upon any of the places aforesaid, out of any boat, lighter, ship, vessel, or bottom, any goods, wares, or merchandise whatsoever, to be brought from any other country, province, or place, or any other part of the said province of the Massachuset's Bay in New England, upon pain of the forfeiture of the said goods, wares, and merchandise, and of the said boat, lighter, ship, or vessel or other bottom into which the same shall be taken, and of the guns, ammunition, tackle, furniture, and stores, in or belonging to the same: And if any such goods, wares, or merchandise, shall, within the said town, or in any the places aforesaid, be laden or taken in from the shore into any barge, hoy, lighter, wherry, or boat, to be carried on board any ship or vessel coming in and arriving from any other country or province, or other part of the said province of the Massachuset's Bay in New England, such barge, hoy, lighter, wherry, or boat, shall be forfeited and lost.

II. And be it further enacted by the authority aforesaid, That if any warfinger, or keeper of any wharf, crane, or quay, of their servants, or any of them, shall take up or land, or knowingly suffer to be taken up or landed, or shall ship off, or suffer to be waterborne, at or from any of their said wharfs, cranes, or quays, any such goods, wares, or merchandise; in every such case, all and every such warfinger, and keeper of such wharf, crane, or quay, and every person whatever who shall be assisting, or otherwise concerned in the shipping or in the loading or putting on board any boat, or other vessel for that purpose, or in the unshipping such goods, wares, and merchandise, or to whose hands the same shall knowingly come after the loading, shipping, or unshipping thereof, shall forfeit and lose treble the value thereof, to be computed at the highest price which such sort of goods, wares, and merchandise, shall bear at the place where such offence shall be committed, together with the vessels and boats, and all the horses, cattle, and carriages, whatsoever made use of in the shipping, unshipping, landing, removing, carriage, or conveyance of any of the aforesaid goods, wares, and merchandise.

III. And be it further enacted by the authority aforesaid, That if any ship or vessel shall be moored or lie at anchor, or be seen hovering within the said bay, described and bounded as aforesaid, or within one league from the said bay so described, or the said headlands, or any of the islands lying between or within the same, it shall and may be lawful for any admiral, chief commander, or commissioned officer, of his Majesty's fleet or ships of war, or for any officer of his Majesty's customs, to compel such ship or vessel to depart to some other port or harbour, or to such station as the said officer shall appoint, and to use such force for that purpose as shall be found necessary: And if such ship or vessel shall not depart accordingly, within six hours after notice for that purpose given by such person as aforesaid, such ship or vessel, together with all the goods laden on board thereon, and all the guns, ammunition, tackle, and furniture, shall be forfeited and lost, whether bulk shall have been broken or not.

IV. Provided always, That nothing in this act contained shall extend, or be construed to extend, to any military or other stores for his Majesty's use, or to the ships or vessels whereon the same shall be laden, which shall be commissioned by, and in the immediate pay of, his Majesty, his heirs or successors; nor to any fuel or victual brought coastwise from any part of the continent of America, for the necessary use and sustenance of the inhabitants of the said town of Boston, provided the vessels wherein the same are to be carried shall be duly furnished with a cocket and let-pass, after having been duly searched by the proper officers of his Majesty's customs at Marblehead, in the port of Salem, in the said province of Massachuset's Bay; and that some officer of his Majesty's customs be also there put on board the said vessel, who is hereby authorized to go on board, and proceed with the said vessel, together with a sufficient number of persons, properly armed, for his defence, to the said town or harbour of Boston; nor to any ships or vessels which may happen to be within the said harbour of Boston on or before the first day of June, one thousand seven hundred and seventy four, and may have either laden or taken on board, or be there with intent to load or take on board, or to land or discharge any goods, wares, and merchandise, provided the said ships and vessels do depart the said harbour within fourteen days after the said first day of June, one thousand seven hundred and seventy-four.

V. And be it further enacted by the authority aforesaid, That all seizures, penalties, and forfeitures, inflicted by this act, shall be made and prosecuted by any admiral, chief commander, or commissioned officer, of his Majesty's fleet, or ships of war, or by the officers of his Majesty's customs, or some of them, or by some other person deputed or authorised, by warrant from the lord high treasurer, or the commissioners of his Majesty's treasury for the time being, and by no other person whatsoever: And if any such officer, or other person authorised as aforesaid, shall, directly or indirectly, take or receive any bribe or reward, to connive at such lading or unlading, or shall make or commence any collusive seizure, information, or agreement for that purpose, or shall do any other act whatsoever, whereby the goods, wares, or merchandise, prohibited as aforesaid, shall be suffered to pass, either inwards or outwards, or whereby the forfeitures and penalties inflicted by this act may be evaded, every such offender shall forfeit the sum of five hundred pounds for every such offence, and shall become incapable of any office or employment, civil or military; and every person who shall give, offer, or promise, any such bribe or reward, or shall contract, agree, or treat with any person, so authorised as aforesaid, to commit any such offfence, shall forfeit the sum of fifty pounds.

VI. And be it further enacted by the authority aforesaid, That the forfeitures and penalties inflicted by this act shall and may be prosecuted, sued for, and recovered, and be divided, paid, and applied, in like manner as other penalties and forfeitures inflicted by any act or acts of parliament, relating to the trade or revenues of the British colonies or plantations in America, are directed to be prosecuted, sued for, or recovered, divided, paid, and applied, by two several acts of parliament, the one passed in the fourth year of his present Majesty, (intituled, (To give a designation or title to (a legislative act, for example). An act for granting certain duties in the British colonies and plantations in America; for continuing, amending, and making perpetual, an act passed in the sixth year of the reign of his late majesty King George the Second, intituled, An act for the better securing and encouraging the trade of his Majesty's sugar colonies in America: for applying the produce of such duties, and of the duties to arise by virtue of the said act, towards defraying the expences of defending, protecting, and securing, the said colonies and plantations; for explaining an act made in the twenty-fifth year of the reign of King Charles the Second, intituled, An act for the encouragement of the Greenland and Eastland trades, and for the better securing the plantation trade; and for altering and disallowing several drawbacks on exports from this kingdom, and more effectually preventing the clandestine conveyance of goods to and from the said colonies and plantations, and improving and securing the trade between the same and Great Britain;) the other passed in the eighth year of his present Majesty's reign, (intituled, An act for the more easy and effectual recovery of the penalties and forfeitures inflicted by the acts of parliament relating to the trade or revenues of the British colonies and plantations in America.)

VII. And be it further enacted by the authority aforesaid, That every charter party bill of loading, and other contract for consigning shipping, or carrying any goods, wares, and merchandize whatsoever, to or from the said town of Boston, or any part of the bay or harbour thereof, described as aforesaid, which have been made or entered into, or which shall be made or entered into, so long as this act shall remain in full force, relating to any ship which shall arrive at the said town or harbour, after the first day of June, one thousand seven hundred and seventy-four, shall be, and the same are hereby declared to be utterly void, to all intents and purposes whatsoever.

VIII. And be it further enacted by the authority aforesaid, That whenever it shall be made to appear to his Majesty, in his privy council, that peace and obedience to the laws shall be so far restored in the said town of Boston, that the trade of Great Britain may safely be carried on there, and his Majesty's customs duly collected, and his Majesty, in his privy council, shall adjudge the same to be true, it shall and may be lawful for his Majesty, by proclamation, or order of council, to assign and appoint the extent, bounds, and limits, of the port or harbour of Boston, and of every creek or haven within the same, or in the islands within the precincts thereof; and also to assign and appoint such and so many open places, quays, and wharfs, within the said harbour, creeks, havens, and islands, for the landing, discharging, lading, and shipping of goods, as his Majesty, his heirs or successors, shall judge necessary and expedient; and also to appoint such and so many officers of the customs therein as his Majesty shall think fit, after which it shall be lawful for any person or persons to lade or put off from, or to discharge and land upon, such wharfs, quays, and places, so appointed within the said harbour, and none other, any goods, wares, and merchandise whatever.

IX. Provided always, That if any goods, wares, or merchandize, shall be laden or put off from, or discharged or landed upon, any other place than the quays, wharfs, or places, so to be appointed, the same, together with the ships, boats, and other vessels employed therein, and the horses, or other cattle and carriages used to convey the same, and the person or persons concerned or assisting therein, or to whose hands the same shall knowingly come, shall suffer all the forfeitures and penalties imposed by this or any other act on the illegal shipping or landing of goods.

X. Provided also, and it is hereby declared and enacted, That nothing herein contained shall extend, or be construed, to enable his Majesty to appoint such port, harbour, creeks, quays, wharfs, places, or officers in the said town of Boston, or in the said bay or islands, until it shall sufficiently appear to his Majesty that full satisfaction hath been made by or on behalf of the inhabitants of the said town of Boston to the united company of merchants of England trading to the East Indies, for the damage sustained by the said company by the destruction of their goods sent to the said town of Boston, on board certain ships or vessels as aforesaid; and until it shall be certified to his Majesty, in council, by the governor, or lieutenant governor, of the said province, that reasonable satisfaction hath been made to the officers of his Majesty's revenue, and others, who suffered by the riots and insurrections above mentioned, in the months of November and December, in the year one thousand seven hundred and seventy-three, and in the month of January, in the year one thousand seven hundred and seventy-four.

XI. And be it further enacted by the authority aforesaid, That if any action or suit shall be commenced, either in Great Britain or America, against any person or persons, for any thing done in pursuance of this act of parliament, the defendant or defendants, in such action or suit, may plead the general issue, and give the said act, and the special matter, in evidence, at any trial to be had thereupon, and that the same was done in pursuance and by the authority of this act: and if it shall appear so to have been done, the jury shall find for the defendant or defendants; and if the plaintiff shall be nonsuited, or discontinue his action, after the defendant or defendants shall have appeared: or if judgment shall be given upon any verdict or demurrer, against the plaintiff, the defendant or defendants shall recover treble costs, and have the like remedy for the same, as defendants have in other cases by law.

Chapter 10

The Olive Branch Petition

(Adapted Text)

The Olive Branch Petition was written by the Continental Congress, a colonial legislature that the British Parliament did not recognize as a rightful governing body. The colonists sent the document to King George III. Sending it seemed like a very reasonable thing to do, because the conflicts between the colonists and England were escalating at an alarming rate.

Below is an olive branch. What do you think the olive branch symbolizes?

The Olive Branch Petition (adapted)

July 8, 1775

To the King's Most Excellent Majesty.

*M*OST GRACIOUS SOVEREIGN: We, your faithful subjects of the Colonies of New-Hampshire, Massachusetts-Bay, Rhode-Island, New-Jersey, Pennsylvania, the Counties of Newcastle, Kent, and Sussex, on Delaware, Maryland, Virginia, North Carolina, and South Carolina, on behalf of the Congress and the citizens of the Colonies, who have authorized us to represent them in General Congress, ask for your Majesty's attention to this simple petition.

*T*he remarkable partnership that has existed between our Mother Country (Britain), with its mild and fair government, and these Colonies, has produced enormous wealth. The benefits of our partnership have been so important and lasting; the other nations have only been able to watch with envy as Great Britain rose to be the greatest power the world has ever known.

*W*ithout any major disagreements in our relationship, Great Britain's enemies grew concerned of the Crown's rising economic wealth and power, and tried stopping the growth of these colonies.

*D*uring this attempt, events so terrible took place that every friend to Great Britain and these Colonies, happily agreed that additional soldiers should come to the colonies and fight for the removal of our ancient and warlike enemies.

*I*n this last war, we loyally contributed repeated and tireless efforts to the most glorious victory ever won by British arms. You, and the last king (George II) often praised our efforts. We all shared in the blessings of peace and victory.

But then, to our astonishment, while this honorable victory was still fresh, parliament passed a new system of statutes and laws to manage the colonies. These laws, passed without a hint or accusation of any wrongdoing by us, created a greater fear of domestic danger than any foreign enemy could.

Furthermore, any short term gains from these new laws would injure the colonies immediately, but would then injure the Mother Country's commerce and prosperity in the long term.

We shall decline the ungrateful task of describing the irksome variety of tactics practiced by many of your Majesty's Ministers: the lies, the terrors, and the severities, that have been dealt out by them in their attempts to carry out this misguided plan. We also decline the task of reminding you of these many differences between Great Britain and these colonies, and the lack of progress that came from these ministers.

Your Majesty's Ministers, constantly trying to uphold these ridiculous measures, even started hostilities to enforce them. This forced us to arm in our own defense. Not only that, these actions then forced us to engage in conversations that were very odd and objectionable to the loyalties of your still faithful Colonists. And, when we have to consider who we are opposing in this disagreement, and the possible consequences if it continues, it causes us even greater distress.

We know that civil conflict can create violent resentments and never-ending hatred. So we believe we have an obligation to Almighty God, your Majesty, our fellow subjects, and to ourselves, to use all the means in our power to stop further bloodshed, and try to avoid the approaching tragedies that threaten the British Empire.

herefore, we are addressing your majesty, and all your dominions, with sincere respect, to consider what is happening in America. Can we fully explain to you what troubles our minds, your dutiful subjects? If our language seems disrespectful, that is not our intention. However, it is hard to remain respectful when we are discussing matters of our own protection from those deceitful and cruel enemies who abuse your confidence and authority, for the purpose of destroying us.

e solemnly promise your Majesty that not only do we want the former relationship we shared to be restored, but a strong foundation that will establish a lasting friendship that can weather future disagreements, will enrich our future generations, multiply our blessings, and elevate your majesty's name to posterity.

e further pledge to your Majesty, even after all the sufferings we have endured during our present arguments; that we have too much respect for this kingdom, from which we trace our roots, to ask for any agreement that might dishonor Great Britain's dignity. Once the complaints, that have been heavy on our hearts, are recognized and cured, our honor, duty, and desire will find us ready and faithful subjects, ready to pledge our lives and our fortunes to your majesty and our Mother Country.

our majesty, we plead with you to use your majestic authority and wisdom to aid in these important issues so that a permanent reconciliation may be found. We ask that you find a way to soothe our fears and jealousies, and prevent the further destruction of the lives of your subjects. For such arrangements from your Majesty's wisdom, your colonists will again offer their continued devotion as loyal and dutiful subjects.

hat your Majesty may enjoy long and prosperous reign, and that your descendants may govern your Dominions with honor to themselves and happiness to their subjects, is our sincere prayer.

Signed by:

Colony of New Hampshire

John Langdon
Thomas Cushing

New Jersey

William Livingston
John De Hart
Richard Smith

Colony of Massachusetts

Samuel Adams
John Adams
Robert Treat Paine

Pennsylvania

John Dickinson
Benjamin Franklin
George Ross
James Wilson
Charles Humphreys
Edward Biddle

Colony of Rhode-Island and the Providence Plantations

Stephen Hopkins
Samuel Ward

Counties of Newcastle, Kent, Sussex [Delaware Counties]

Caesar Rodney
Thomas Mckean
George Read

Colony of Connecticut

Eliphalet Dyer
Roger Sherman
Silas Deane

Maryland

Matthew Tilghman
Thomas Johnson, Jr.
William Paca
Samuel Chase
Thomas Stone

Colony of New York

Philip Livingston
James Duane
John Alsop
Francis Lewis
John Jay
Robert Livingston, Jr.
Lewis Morris
William Floyd
Henry Wisner

The Olive Branch Petition
(Original Text)

July 8, 1775

To the King's Most Excellent Majesty.

MOST GRACIOUS SOVEREIGN: We, your Majesty's faithful subjects of the Colonies of New-Hampshire, Massachusetts-Bay, Rhode-Island, New-Jersey, Pennsylvania, the Counties of Newcastle, Kent, and Sussex, on Delaware, Maryland, Virginia, North Carolina, and South Carolina, in behalf of ourselves and the inhabitants of these Colonies, who have deputed us to represent them in General Congress, entreat your Majesty's gracious attention to this our humble petition.

The union between our Mother Country and these Colonies, and the energy of mild and just Government, produce benefits so remarkably important, and afforded such an assurance of their permanency and increase, that the wonder and envy of other nations were excited, while they beheld Great Britain rising to a power the most extra-ordinary the world had ever known.

Her rivals, observing that there was no probability of this happy connexion being broken by civil dissensions, and apprehending its future effects if left any longer undisturbed, resolved to prevent her receiving such continual and formidable accessions of wealth and strength, by checking the growth of those settlements from which they were to be derived.

In the prosecution of this attempt, events so unfavourable to the design took place, that every friend to the interests of Great Britain and these Colonies, entertained pleasing and reasonable expectations of seeing an additional force and exertion immediately given to the operations of the union hitherto experienced, by an enlargement of the dominions of the Crown, and the removal of ancient and warlike enemies to a greater distance.

At the conclusion, therefore, of the late war, the most glorious and advantageous that ever had been carried on by British arms, your loyal Colonists having contributed to its success by such repeated and strenuous exertions as frequently procured them the distinguished approbation of your Majesty, of the late King, and of Parliament, doubted not but that they should be permitted, with the rest of the Empire, to share in the blessings of peace, and the emoluments of victory and conquest.

While these recent and honourable acknowledgements of their merits remained on record in the Journals and acts of that august Legislature, the Parliament, undefaced by the imputation or even the suspicion of any offence, they were alarmed by a new system of statutes and regulations adopted for the administration of the Colonies, that filled their minds with the most painful fears and jealousies; and, to their inexpressible astonishment, perceived the danger of a foreign quarrel quickly succeeded by domestick danger, in their judgment of a more dreadful kind.

Nor were these anxieties alleviated by any tendency in this system to promote the welfare of their Mother Country. For though its effects were more immediately felt by them, yet its influence appeared to be injurious to the commerce and prosperity of Great Britain.

We shall decline the ungrateful task of describing the irksome variety of artifices practised by many of your Majesty's Ministers, the delusive pretences, fruitless terrours, and unavailing severities, that have, from time to time, been dealt out by them, in their attempts to execute this impolitick plan, or of tracing through a series of years past the progress of the unhappy differences between Great Britain and these Colonies, that have flowed from this fatal source.

Your Majesty's Ministers, persevering in their measures, and proceeding to open hostilities for enforcing them, have compelled us to arm in our own defence, and have engaged us in a controversy so peculiarly abhorrent to the affections of your still faithful Colonists, that when we consider whom we must oppose in this contest, and if it continues, what may be the consequences, our own particular misfortunes are accounted by us only as parts of our distress.

Knowing to what violent resentments and incurable animosities civil discords are apt to exasperate and inflame the contending parties, we think ourselves required by indispensable obligations to Almighty God, to your Majesty, to our fellow-subjects, and to ourselves, immediately to use all the means in our power, not incompatible with our safety, for stopping the further effusion of blood, and for averting the impending calamities that threaten the British Empire.

Thus called upon to address your Majesty on affairs of such moment to America, and probably to all your Dominions, we are earnestly desirous of performing this office with the utmost deference for your Majesty; and we therefore pray, that your Majesty's royal magnanimity and benevolence may make the most favourable constructions of our expressions on so uncommon an occasion. Could we represent in their full force the sentiments that agitate the minds of us your dutiful subjects, we are persuaded your Majesty would ascribe any seeming deviation from reverence in our language, and even in our conduct, not to any reprehensible intention, but to the impossibility of reconciling the usual appearance of respect with a just attention to our own preservation against those artful and cruel enemies who abuse your royal confidence and authority, for the purpose of effecting our destruction.

*A*ttached to your Majesty's person, family, and Government, with all devotion that principle and affection can inspire; connected with Great Britain by the strongest ties that can unite societies, and deploring every event that tends in any degree to weaken them, we solemnly assure your Majesty, that we not only most ardently desire the former harmony between her and these Colonies may be restored, but that a concord may be established between them upon so firm a basis as to perpetuate its blessings, uninterrupted by any future dissensions, to succeeding generations in both countries, and to transmit your Majesty's name to posterity, adorned with that signal and lasting glory that has attended the memory of those illustrious personages, whose virtues and abilities have extricated states from dangerous convulsions, and by securing the happiness to others, have erected the most noble and durable monuments to their own fame.

*W*e beg further leave to assure your Majesty, that notwithstanding the sufferings of your loyal Colonists during the course of this present controversy, our breasts retain too tender a regard for the kingdom from which we derive our origin, to request such a reconciliation as might, in any manner, be inconsistent with her dignity or welfare. These, related as we are to her, honour and duty, as well as inclination, induce us to support and advance; and the apprehensions that now oppress our hearts with unspeakable grief, being once removed, your Majesty will find our faithful subject on this Continent ready and willing at all times, as they have ever been with their lives and fortunes, to assert and maintain the rights and interests of your Majesty, and of our Mother Country.

*W*e therefore beseech your Majesty, that your royal authority and influence may be graciously interposed to procure us relief from our afflicting fears and jealousies, occasioned by the system before-mentioned, and to settle peace through every part of our Dominions, with all humility submitting to your Majesty's wise consideration, whether it may not be expedient, for facilitating those important purposes, that your Majesty be pleased to direct some mode, by which the united applications of your faithful Colonists to the Throne, in pursuance of their common counsels, may be improved into a happy and permanent reconciliation; and that, in the mean time, measures may be taken for preventing the further destruction of the lives of your Majesty's subjects; and that such statutes as more immediately distress any of your Majesty's Colonies may be repealed.

For such arrangements as your Majesty's wisdom can form for collecting the united sense of your American people, we are convinced your Majesty would receive such satisfactory proofs of the disposition of the Colonists towards their Sovereign and Parent State, that the wished for opportunity would soon be restored to them, of evincing the sincerity of their professions, by every testimony of devotion becoming the most dutiful subjects, and the most affectionate Colonists.

That your Majesty may enjoy long and prosperous reign, and that your descendants may govern your Dominions with honour to themselves and happiness to their subjects, is our sincere prayer.

King George III

Source: John J. Anderson, *A School History of England* (Effingham Maynard & Co., 1889)

Chapter 11

A Proclamation, by the King, for Suppressing Rebellion and Sedition

Proclamation, by the King, for Suppressing Rebellion and Sedition—King George III's response to The Olive Branch Petition and "the traitors" in the colonies.

In fact, it really wasn't much of an answer at all. As kings usually did, they simply announced their views and expected others to accept them. This "answer" to the colonists was merely a proclamation—a formal public statement. To the surprise of many colonists, the king refused to accept the Olive Branch Petition while he was on the throne.

Now that you have had a chance to read the Olive Branch Petition, why do you think the king's response surprised some of the drafters of that document?

*   *   *

Proclamation, by The King, for
Suppressing Rebellion and Sedition

(Adapted Text)

King George III

August 23, 1775

hereas, there are many of our subjects, in various parts of our North American Colonies and Plantations, who have been misled by dangerous and scheming men; and have forgotten their loyalty, which they owe, to the power that has protected and supported them. After various disorderly acts, disturbing the public peace, the preventing of lawful **commerce**, and abusing our loyal subjects; they have committed open and declared **rebellion** by acting in a hostile manner, breaking the law, and traitorously planning and waging war against us.

> **Rebellion:** Organized, open, and armed resistance to the ruling establishment or government.

owever, since none of our subjects may ignore or disobey their duty, either through ignorance or by doubting that the Crown would reward

> **Sedition:** Resisting authority with the intent to hinder or overthrow the government.

their loyalty, and because there is reason to believe that this rebellion has been greatly encouraged by the traitorous writings and guidance of various evil and desperate people within this kingdom, we have decided, along with the advice of our **Privy Council**, to issue our Royal Proclamation hereby declaring: that all our civil and military officers shall do everything in their power to stop this rebellion and bring the traitors to justice. Furthermore, all the subjects of this Realm, including all its **dominions**, are required by law to help in stopping this rebellion.

> **Privy Council**: The private counselors selected by the monarch (king).
>
> **Dominions**: One of the self-governing nations within Great Britain's influence.

Additionally, because of the traitorous plots against our crown and dignity, we command all our military and civil officers, and all other loyal subjects, to use every means to defend against and suppress such rebellion, and communicate to the Crown all treasons and traitorous schemes which they learn of. When persons have been identified as having communicated with, or helped, those in open rebellion against our Government, their identities are to be passed on to one of our main Secretaries of State, so that the authors, perpetrators, and supporters of such traitorous plans will receive proper punishment.

Given at our Court at St. James's the twenty-third day of August, one thousand seven hundred and seventy-five, in the fifteenth year of our reign.

GOD save the KING.

*   *   *

A Proclamation, by The King, for Suppressing Rebellion and Sedition

(Original Text)

King George III

August 23, 1775

Whereas many of our subjects in divers parts of our Colonies and Plantations in North America, misled by dangerous and ill designing men, and forgetting the allegiance which they owe to the power that has protected and supported them; after various disorderly acts committed in disturbance of the publick peace, to the obstruction of lawful commerce, and to the oppression of our loyal subjects carrying on the same; have at length proceeded to open and avowed rebellion, by arraying themselves in a hostile manner, to withstand the execution of the law, and traitorously preparing, ordering and levying war against us: And whereas, there is reason to apprehend that such rebellion hath been much promoted and encouraged by the traitorous correspondence, counsels and comfort of divers wicked and desperate persons within this Realm: To the end therefore, that none of our subjects may neglect or violate their duty through ignorance thereof, or through any doubt of the protection which the law will afford to their loyalty and zeal, we have thought fit, by and with the advice of our Privy Council, to issue our Royal Proclamation, hereby declaring, that not only all our Officers, civil and military, are obliged to exert their utmost endeavours to suppress such rebellion, and to bring the traitors to justice, but that all our subjects of this Realm, and the dominions thereunto belonging, are bound by law to be aiding and assisting in the suppression of such rebellion, and to disclose and make known all traitorous conspiracies and attempts against us, our crown and dignity; and we do accordingly strictly charge and command all our Officers, as well civil as military, and all others our obedient and loyal subjects, to use their utmost endeavours to withstand and suppress such rebellion, and to disclose and make known all treasons and traitorous conspiracies which they shall know to be against us, our crown and dignity; and for that purpose, that they transmit to one of our principal Secretaries of State, or other proper officer, due and full information of all persons who shall be found carrying on correspondence with, or in any manner or degree aiding or abetting the persons now in open arms and rebellion against our Government, within any of our Colonies and Plantations in North America, in order to bring to condign punishment the authors, perpetrators, and abetters of such traitorous designs.

*G*iven at our Court at St. James's the twenty-third day of August, one thousand seven hundred and seventy-five, in the fifteenth year of our reign.

*G*OD save the KING.

"If we are forced to take up guns, if every one of us must become a soldier, we need to permanently remove the control of the King over us."

— adapted from *Common Sense*

SECTION IV

*Fourteen Activities for the Classroom,
or Just for Fun!*

Each of these activities is based upon National Curriculum Standards. Adjust them for your younger or older students, as needed.

"England belongs to Europe; America belongs to itself."

— adapted from *Common Sense*

Guided Reading Questions for

The Elementary Common Sense of

Thomas Paine

Common Sense Activities for the Well Read Student

Introduction, Timeline, and Chapter 1

1. Why do you think Thomas Paine titled his pamphlet "Common Sense?"

2. The illustration right before Thomas Paine's biography shows a young colonist looking at a sign that points in opposite directions. If you were the person in that picture, what would you be thinking? Which path would you choose?

3. In the Introduction are these words: "The founding fathers were like you and me, with extraordinary beliefs in the common good for their fellow citizens." What do you think that means?

4. In the Introduction is a picture of Thomas Paine and King George III. If you were a colonist viewing these two pictures, which person would appeal to you more? Why?

5. Find the years 1754 and 1775 on the timeline. Why would the Continental Congress be interested in creating peace treaties with neighboring Indian tribes?

6. *Common Sense* was originally printed as a pamphlet. In those days, that meant it did not have a cover like a book or magazine has today. Its binding was not sewn or glued, but instead tied together with either coarse string or leather. This made it affordable to publish, which meant it could be sold cheaply so that most people could afford to buy a copy. Why was this important?

7. According to Thomas Paine, "It is the pride of kings that throws mankind into confusion." What do you think he was trying to say about kings? How could having too much pride disrupt the lives of others?

*   *   *

Chapter 2

Guided Reading Questions for
The Elementary Common Sense of Thomas Paine

1. In Chapter 2, Thomas Paine wrote the following: "Youngsters can be taken advantage of, or betrayed." Do you think a young king could be taken advantage of? How?

2. Today, how old do you have to be to before you can be president? Senator? Representative? Governor? Why do you think the framers (those men who wrote our Constitution) put in minimum ages to run for office? (Use an almanac for help if you need one.)

3. In absolute monarchies, Paine reminds us that kings are in charge of everything: business, civilian, and military affairs. This was true even if they had no experience in one or all of these areas. If you could only choose one of these areas (business, civilian, or military), which would be the most important for the monarch to have personal experience in? Why do you think so?

4. At the end of Chapter 2, we learn how much money the king is paid each year. What do you think a king spends his money on?

5. Look once more at the portraits of King George III and Thomas Paine. Which of the them would you borrow a winter coat from? Why?

6. In 1776, Kings lived in palaces and/or castles. Visualize the King's office. What does it look like? Draw a picture or cartoon of the king in his office.

*   *   *

Chapter 3

Guided Reading Questions for
The Elementary Common Sense of Thomas Paine

1. Read this line from Thomas Paine's text: "This is not a cause for a day, a year, or an age, but forever." Why does Paine want to convince the colonists this needs to be a cause that will last forever? What would happen if the king agreed to give the colonists what they wanted?

2. According to Paine, "We have a duty to mankind to end our relationship (with Britain)." Would you have agreed with Paine? Why or why not?

3. "We just flatter arrogant kings . . . with our repeated petitions." One of the petitions he refers to is The Olive Branch Petition (see page 85 to read this document). What do you think Paine meant by this statement?

4. Paine says the King "thirsts for unchecked power." What is "unchecked power," and why would a King want it?

5. Look at the drawing on page 43. In 1776, why do you think it was important for new citizens to immigrate to the colonies?

6. Paine refers to the colonies as perfect equals, and being equal creates no jealously. Do you agree with that statement? Why or why not?

7. "Everyone in the colonies no longer feels close to the British government. They feel more like a teenager preparing to leave home." Why would Paine use an analogy like this? Now, more than two centuries later, can you identify with that statement? How so?

 8. According to Paine, "Europe is too thickly planted with kingdoms." Paine loved comparisons. What other metaphors can you find in this chapter?

*   *   *

Chapter 4

Guided Reading Questions for
The Elementary Common Sense of Thomas Paine

1. How could forming and maintaining a colonial army create new trade (commerce) for the colonies?

2. According to Paine, "The rich are, in general, slaves to fear." How could being rich enslave a person to fear?

3. Look at the photos of the coins on pages 61-62. After the War of Independence (the American Revolution) was won, George Washington was elected as our first president. However, he refused to allow his face to be put on the nation's new coins. Why do you suppose he made that decision?

4. Compare and Contrast the "Olive Branch Petition" and Paine's *Common Sense*. Where do the documents agree? What are some of the major differences between the two documents? (You can use the Venn Diagram on pages 151-152 for help.)

5. Look at 1772 in the timeline. Sam Adams created the Committees of Correspondence. Why was this event so important in colonial America? What might have happened in the coming years if this had not been formed?

6. Read the Boston Port Act (pages 75 - 84). The King closed Boston's port and harbor until the citizens "calmed down" and paid for the tea they destroyed during the Boston Tea Party. Why do you think the colonists didn't settle down after this Act closed the harbor?

7. Visualize how Thomas Paine lived. What did his home look like? What sort of furniture did he have? What sort of personal belongings did he own? Draw a picture of Thomas' house and label the items you think you would find inside it.

Book Club Questions for

The Elementary Common Sense

of Thomas Paine

1. In the beginning of *Common Sense*, Paine spends a lot of time setting the tone for the rest of the book by explaining the differences between a society and a government. What tone is Paine trying to set for the rest of the book? Try to summarize what his purpose is in establishing this difference.

2. In establishing the origins of kings, Paine believes there are only three ways kings could have come into being. Do you agree? Can you think of other circumstances where a monarchy could be established besides the three ways Paine describes?

3. Hereditary Succession in Eighteenth-century England was not just reserved for kings. Members of the House of Lords also passed down their power to their heirs. Why do you think Paine only attacks the monarchy?

4. According to Paine, "We have a duty to mankind to end our relationship (with Britain)." Why is it a duty to mankind instead of only a duty to the colonists?

5. By the end of Chapter 2, Paine has spilled a lot of ink attacking the monarchy. Pretend you are a critic of breaking away from England. Can you think of something positive about having or keeping a king?

6. In *Common Sense*, Paine theorized that only a small portion of Britain's navy and troops would be available to put down the revolution. In reality, the force that Britain sent was the largest ever sent for any military action up to that time. Do you think the discrepancy was intentional, or did Paine just completely underestimate the numbers? Why or why not?

7. The illustration opposite the biography of Thomas Paine near the front of this book shows a young colonist looking at a sign that points to opposite directions. If you were the person in that picture, what would you be thinking?

8. In the Introduction are these words: "The founding fathers were like you and me, with extraordinary beliefs in the common good for their fellow citizens . . ." What do you think that means?

9. *Common Sense* was originally printed as a pamphlet, without a cover like a book or magazine has today, and was tied together with either coarse string or leather. This made it affordable to publish, which meant it could be sold cheaply so that most people could afford to buy a copy. Why was this important? Do you think this was the author's purpose?

10. In absolute monarchies, Paine reminds us that kings are in charge of everything: business, civilian, and military affairs. This was true even if they had no experience in one or all of these areas. If you could only choose one of these areas (business, civilian, or military), which would be the most important for the monarch to have personal experience in? Why do you think so?

Rattle Watch (Police)
Composite of George III

Common Sense Activities for the Two-faced

You get to be a Police Sketch Artist!

✓ Review the list of terms used in this lesson in the back glossary;

✓ Use supplied facial features and do a "police composite" of George III based on Paine's description.

Rattle Watch: Colonists during the Dutch era (1609-1664) who patrolled from sunset until dawn. They carried weapons, lanterns and wooden rattles like this one.

Download this <u>and other free activities</u> in 8.5 x 11 pdf formats at
www.newcommonsensebook.com!

Throughout *Common Sense*, Thomas Paine uses several negative terms in reference to the King and his peers. Some of them include:

Evil   / Royal Brute / Miscreant / Parasites / Barbarous Bully / Savage manners / Hard hearted King / Cruelty of a monster

After reading Paine's description of George III, design what you think the King looked like! On the next page is an empty face with a crown. Use the features on the pages that follow and either cut and paste them in or draw them onto the image. *Make a copy of the next page before you begin so you can experiment over and over on King George III!*

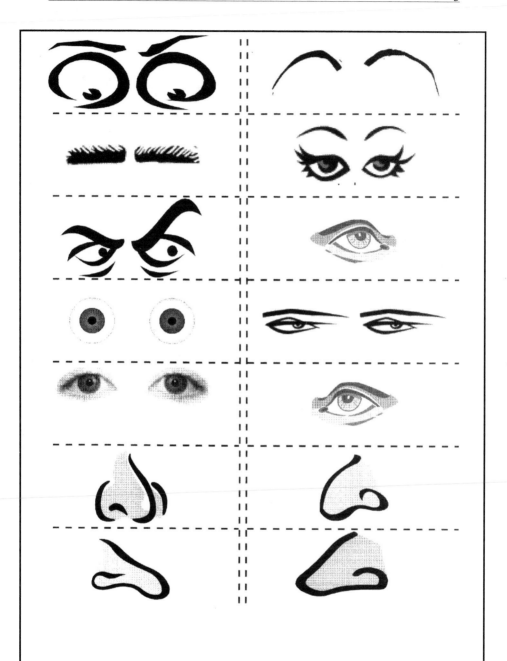

Download this and other free activities in 8.5 x 11 pdf formats at
www.newcommonsensebook.com!

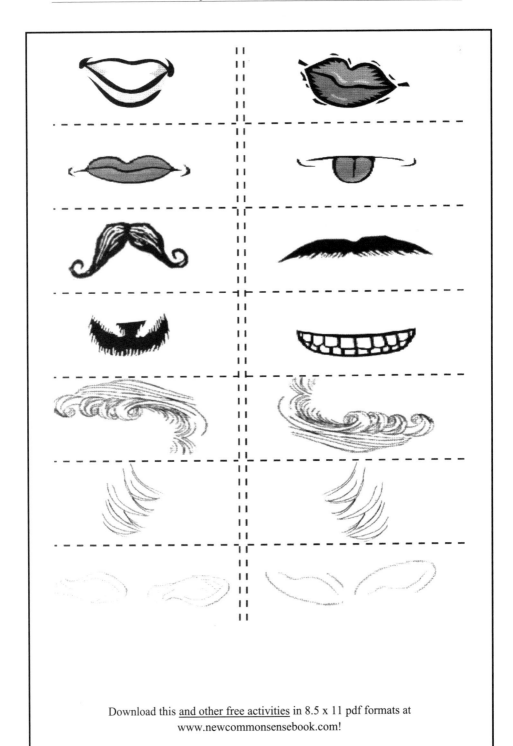

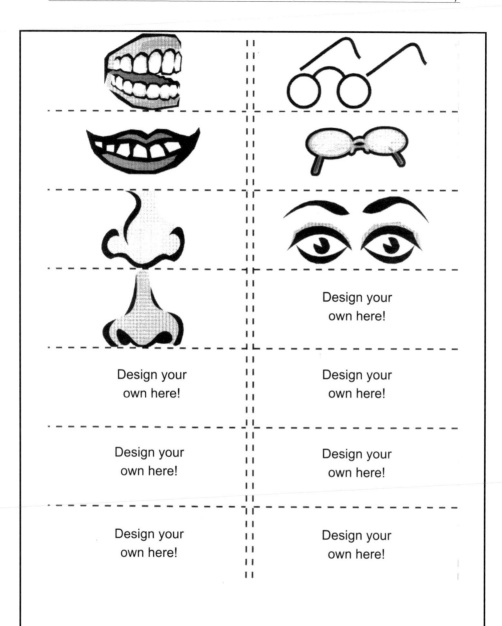

Design your own here!

Design your own here!

Design your own here!

Design your own here!

Design your own here!

Design your own here!

Design your own here!

*D*id you enjoy creating different faces for King George III? Now its time to try the online interactive computer version on our website at www.newcommonsensebook.com.

Click over to our website and try your hand at making a completely different King George III!

Name: _____

A Regal Response

(A letter from King George III after reading Thomas Paine's Common Sense)

What if King George III had read *Common Sense?* Maybe he would have admitted Mr. Paine made some good points. Perhaps he would have been amazed that Mr. Paine wrote some things that just weren't true (and maybe even a bit hurtful). You get to decide.

Pretend you are King George III and write Mr. Paine a letter. How would you respond to *Common Sense*? Remember, kings were used to getting their way, but they usually tried to act in a "kingly" way. If you were king, what would you write to Thomas Paine?

Dear Mr. Paine,

_____

_____

_____

_____

_____

_____

_____

_____

_____

_____

_____

_____

_____

_____

_____

_____

Sincerely,

George III
Your King of Great Britain

The Closing of the Port:
Cause & Effect
Inference Activity

Common Sense Activities

for the Seasick

✓ Read: The Port Act (page 75)

✓ Review Situation Map (page 2)

Boston Harbor was the center of commerce for Massachusetts. Its closure created significant hardships for many people—and not just the folks who lived in and around Boston. Try to imagine the effects that the closing of the large port of Boston would have had on the following people.

How would their life change if the port was closed?

A Dockworker?

A Wharf Owner?

An Importer?

An Exporter?

A Shop Owner?

An Apprentice at the Local Newspaper?

A Street Sweeper?

A Tavern Owner?

On someone who sells carriages and horses?

On a British Regular Soldier stationed in Boston?

On an Importer in England?

On an Exporter in England?

Persuasive Writing Nugget Hunt

Common Sense Activities
for Treasure Seekers

Thomas Paine wrote *Common Sense* to persuade colonists they needed to separate from Great Britain, declare their independence from the King, and become "Americans."

Review **the adapted *Common Sense***. Can you find examples where Thomas Paine used these seven (7) persuasive elements?

1. Appeals to logic

2. Appeals to emotion

3. Appeals to reason

4. Appeals to a higher cause or purpose

5. Uses comparisons

6. Exaggerates

7. States opinion as fact

1) *Appeals to Logic:*

Sentence _____

_____

_____

Chapter: _____ Page: _____

2) *Appeals to Emotion:*

Sentence _____

_____

_____

Chapter: _____ Page: _____

3) *Appeals to Reason:*

Sentence _____

_____

_____

Chapter: _____ Page: _____

4) *Appeals to a Higher Cause or Purpose:*

Sentence _____

_____

_____

Chapter: _____ Page: _____

---

5) *Uses Comparisons:*

Sentence _____

_____

_____

Chapter: _____ Page: _____

---

6) *An Exaggeration:*

Sentence _____

_____

_____

Chapter: _____ Page: _____

---

7) *States Opinion as Fact:*

Sentence _____

_____

_____

Chapter: _____ Page: _____

Fact or Opinion?

Common Sense Activities
for the Opinionated

Name: _____

Thomas Paine's *Common Sense*, is an expertly written pamphlet that includes plenty of facts, and plenty of Thomas' own opinions. A good writer can combine the two almost seamlessly in a persuasive essay. However, as a reader—and an independent learner—you need to be able to tell the difference between fact and opinion. Can you provide examples of both?

FACT	OPINION
(For example) Chapter 3: Men from all walks of life have involved themselves in this argument.	(For example) Weapons must decide this contest.
(For example) …Great Britain has protected us.	(For example) …she would have defended anyone for profits and power.

FACT	OPINION

1776 Government Vocabulary Sort

Cut out these cards for center activity or small group word work.

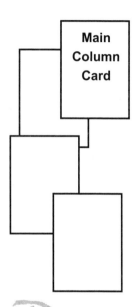

Main Column Card

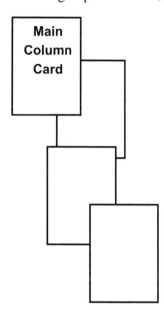

Main Column Card

*P*aine spends much of *Common Sense* trying to convince his readers that the government in Great Britain (the monarchy) was flawed. He used many terms to illustrate his point. He also used other terms to guide his readers to a new way of thinking: **individual freedoms** and **rights**.

Using the glossary found in the back of the book, have students sort vocabulary cards between the two different column cards. Note: students might be able to successfully argue that some terms can be used in both columns.

Governments and Abuses of Power MAIN COLUMN CARD	Ideas and Actions that Empower Citizens MAIN COLUMN CARD
1776 Government Vocabulary Sort **MONARCHS**	1776 Government Vocabulary Sort **TYRANNY**
1776 Government Vocabulary Sort **SUBJECTS**	1776 Government Vocabulary Sort **ASSEMBLIES**
1776 Government Vocabulary Sort **SOVEREIGN**	1776 Government Vocabulary Sort **STATUTES**

Download this <u>and other free activities</u> in 8.5 x 11 pdf formats at
www.newcommonsensebook.com!

1776 Government
Vocabulary Sort

TYRANT

1776 Government
Vocabulary Sort

CONSTITUTION

1776 Government
Vocabulary Sort

MILITIA

1776 Government
Vocabulary Sort

INSURRECTION

1776 Government
Vocabulary Sort

DOMINIONS

1776 Government
Vocabulary Sort

CROWN

1776 Government
Vocabulary Sort

CHECK

1776 Government
Vocabulary Sort

DOMINATE

1776 Government Vocabulary Sort **OPPRESSION**	776 Government Vocabulary Sort **ABSOLUTE MONARCHY**
1776 Government Vocabulary Sort **REPRESENTATIVE**	1776 Government Vocabulary Sort **REPEAL**
1776 Government Vocabulary Sort **ABSOLUTE**	1776 Government Vocabulary Sort **KING**
1776 Government Vocabulary Sort **HOSTILITIES**	1776 Government Vocabulary Sort **INDIVIDUALITY**

1776 Government
Vocabulary Sort

PUBLIC SPEECH

1776 Government
Vocabulary Sort

WARSHIPS

1776 Government
Vocabulary Sort

(Can you think of another?)

_____

1776 Government
Vocabulary Sort

(Can you think of another?)

_____

1776 Government
Vocabulary Sort

(Can you think of another?)

_____

1776 Government
Vocabulary Sort

(Can you think of another?)

_____

1776 Government
Vocabulary Sort

(Can you think of another?)

_____

1776 Government
Vocabulary Sort

(Can you think of another?)

_____

Should the King Declare War?

Common Sense Activities for the Revolutionary Student

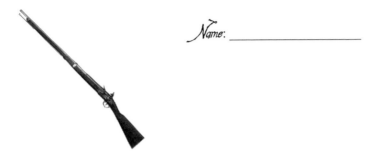

Name: _____

✓ Read: "The Olive Branch Petition" (page 85)
✓ Read: "A Proclamation for Rebellion and Sedition" (page 97)
✓ Review: Timeline (pages 3-8)

The colonists are not backing down from their demands and complaints (but they do want to stay British). A majority of the colonists are not even *considering* independence—even in 1775! They believe Parliament is to blame for most of the quarrels, and they are still very loyal to the king. However, after receiving The "Olive Branch Petition," the King essentially declares war against his own colonies!

You be king for a while. Write down all the pros and cons you can think of before declaring war on your own citizens across the Atlantic Ocean. The first line is filled in to help you get started.

Did King George III make the right decision?

Reasons For Declaring War	Reasons Against Declaring War
Colonists are destroying tea	Colonists are still British Citizens

Reasons For Declaring War	Reasons Against Declaring War

Write your own
"Common Sense" Pamphlet

Common Sense Writing Activities for Rabble Rousers

Name: _____

*T*homas Paine wrote *Common Sense* to persuade colonists that they needed to split from Great Britain, declare independence, and become "Americans." That is the key element in persuasive writing—convincing readers to agree with your point of view. *Common Sense* came out as a pamphlet. Because it had no cover or binding, it was affordable to publish and could be sold cheaply so that most people could afford to buy a copy. (Why do you think that was important?)

To influence the reader, elements of persuasive essays contain the following techniques:

Appeal to logic

Appeal to emotion

Appeal to reason

Appeal to a higher cause or purpose

Use comparisons

Exaggerate

State opinion as fact

Pick something you want changed. Maybe you want microwaves in the cafeteria, all-natural organic candy bars in the vending machines, or a four-day school week instead of five. The sky's the limit. Pick something you want changed, sharpen your quill, and begin writing!

Download this <u>and other free activities</u> in 8.5 x 11 pdf formats at
www.newcommonsensebook.com!

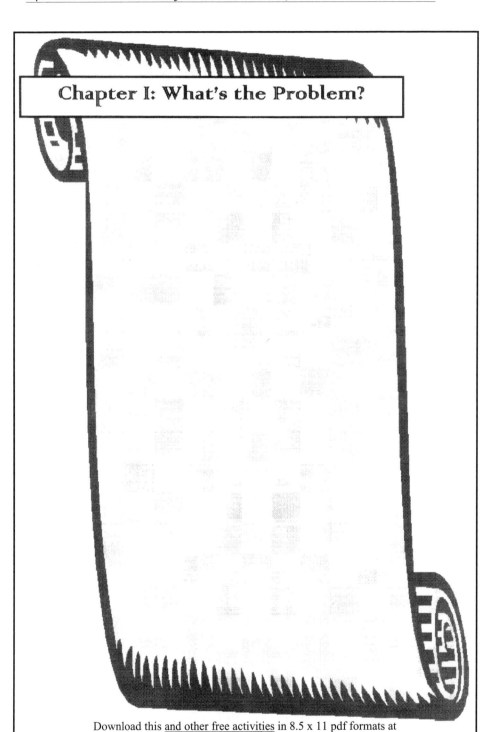

Chapter I: What's the Problem?

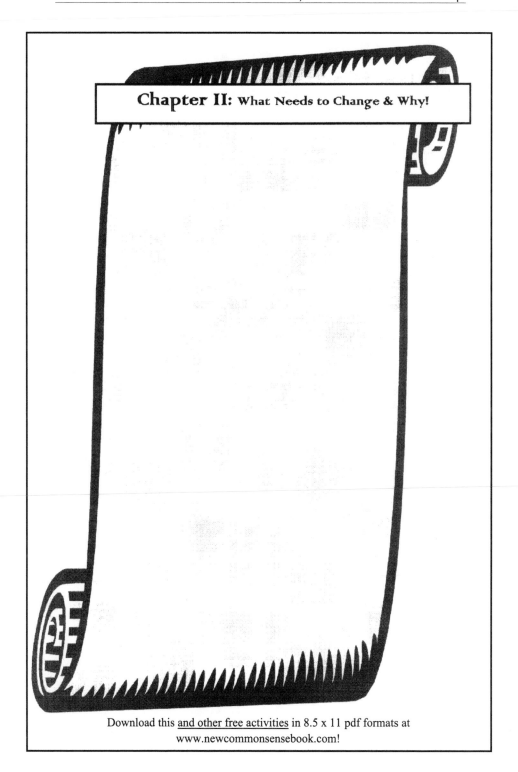

Chapter II: What Needs to Change & Why!

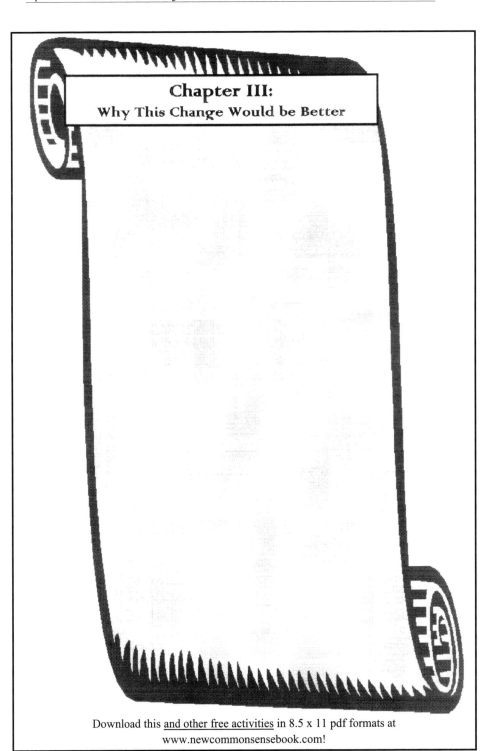

Chapter III:
Why This Change Would be Better

The British Invasion of New York 1776

Common Sense Math for Boatswains

Name: _____

~Math Lesson~

Look at the tables on pages 49-50, in which Thomas Paine records the cost of British ships in 1776.

It was estimated that 30,000 British Regular troops landed in and around New York City in June, July, and August of 1776. Ships "as far as the eye could see," noted many eyewitnesses, were reported in the waters around New York.

Can you calculate the value of these British ships on that eventful day?

* Answers can be found on page 195.

Download this <u>and other free activities</u> in 8.5 x 11 pdf formats at www.newcommonsensebook.com!

For questions 1-4 below, use Paine's tables on pages 49-50 and calculate the value of the following ships and guns:

1) 20 Frigates with 60 guns = _____

2) 16 Frigates with 50 guns = _____

3) 4 Frigates with 90 guns = _____

4) 40 Frigates with 20 guns = _____

5) Total of all 80 Frigates (1 – 4 above) = _____

For questions 6-10 below, determine how to set the problem up, and then solve it.

6) A British landing craft can carry 20 soldiers from a frigate to shore every 30 minutes (half-hour). How many soldiers can one landing craft carry in six hours?

7) How many soldiers can be taken to shore by 100 landing craft in six hours? _____

8) In the first questions in this section (1-5 above), there were a total of 80 frigates involved. If there were five landing craft for every frigate, how many total landing craft were there?

9) Using information from the previous questions, answer this: If each frigate needs to land 300 men, and there is only one landing craft per frigate, how many trips will each landing craft have to make to shore in order to land all 300 men?

10) How many total trips will landing craft make to land 30,000 troops?

Design the First Coin

Common Sense Activities for Common Cents

Name: _____

✓ Review Coins of the Colonies (page 61)

✓ Review Mercantilism (page 65)

The War of Independence is now over and we have become the United States of America, (instead of the United Colonies). One of the many things we need to do is create our own money. However, President Washington will not allow his face on the new money (why do you think he made that decision?). What should the new coins look like? What symbols would YOU use? Think about the reasons colonists had to declare independence and themes Paine wrote about in Common Sense.

Look at money today—what is similar about the different coins? What symbols do you see? Create a coin that communicates what the new country is thinking about. Include a key explaining any symbols you use (and don't forget to include the value).

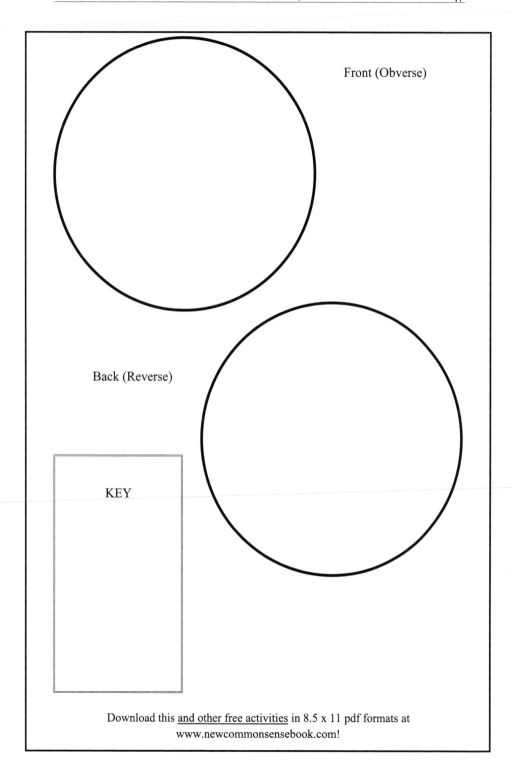

Front (Obverse)

Back (Reverse)

KEY

Download this <u>and other free activities</u> in 8.5 x 11 pdf formats at
www.newcommonsensebook.com!

National Park Webquest (Pre-1776)

Common Sense Activities for Park Enthusiasts

:

_____

1)

Fort Necessity 1754:
http://www.nps.gov/fone/historyculture/index.htm
This famous person was only 22 years old when the first military event in his career occurred. Who is this person?

2)

Old Fort Western: http://www.oldfortwestern.org/afortbeth.html, the staging area for the siege on Quebec. Click on **Fort History**. How long did Benedict Arnold and his men stay at this fort before heading toward Canada? Also, check out September 1775 on the Timeline, p. 7.

3)

Dorchester Heights:
http://www.nps.gov/archive/bost/Dorchester_Heights.htm
How many cannon were taken from Fort Ticonderoga to Dorchester Heights around Boston, and then aimed at the British troops stationed in that important colonial city? (See also the map printed on page 2.)

4)

Paul Revere's House:
http://www.nps.gov/bost/historyculture/prh.htm
Click on: "For more information visit the Paul Revere House," then "The Midnight Ride Learn More," and finally "The Real Story of the Midnight Ride." Which two men was Paul Revere sent to warn?

5)

Old North Church: http://www.oldnorth.com/   Once of the most popular slogans to come out of the American Revolution is "One if by land, two if by sea." Click on "History and Architecture." Who gave the church the silver that is used in its services?"

6)

Thomas Paine Monument: http://www.jhdougherty.com/paine/. Here, finally, is a monument to the author of *Common Sense*—Thomas Paine! Click on "Thomas Paine Memorial . . ." Finish this sentence written by Paine: "These are the times . . ."

7)

Biography of King George III:
http://www.royal.gov.uk/output/Page111.asp (Not an NPS website, but it is a cool website worth visiting.) What are some of the expenses the king was suppose to pay with his annual grant?

8)

Paul Revere's Midnight Ride:
http://www.paulreverehouse.org/ride/virtual.shtml
Here is a virtual ride of the Revere and Dawes ride. Find the colonial mile marker image. What was the name of the town Revere passed through that is now call Arlington?

* Answer Key, page 195

Venn Diagram: Compare & Contrast

Common Sense Activities for Petitioners

*N*ame: _____

✓   Use with Guided Reading Question 4, Chapter 4

*O*n the facing page is a Venn diagram to compare and contrast Thomas Paine's *Common Sense* with the Olive Branch Petition. Are there similarities that overlap? What major points of each document *do not* overlap?

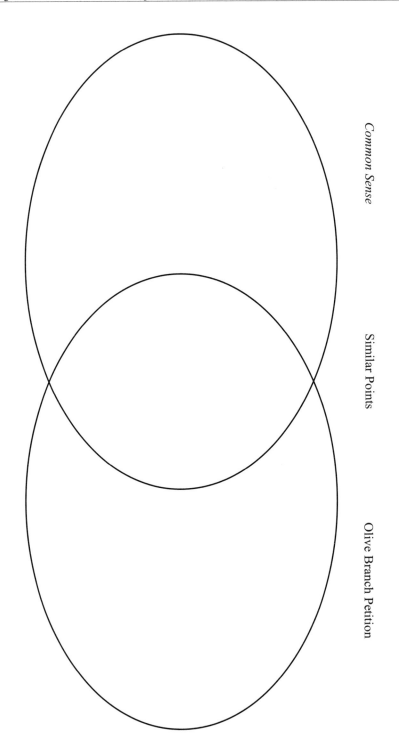

Common Sense

Similar Points

Olive Branch Petition

SECTION V

Thomas Paine in the British Press

"I rejected the hardened, sullen tempered
Pharaoh of England for ever. . ."

— Thomas Paine

British Cartoons about

Thomas Paine

✓ Review Paine's Activities after the Revolution (pages 1-2, 58).

Two of the cartoons that follow were drawn by James Gillray (1756-1815), a political cartoonist who lived in Great Britain. Gillray sometimes published his work under the nickname, "for the public good."

These particular cartoons were drawn in the 1790s—two decades after the American Revolution began. Study them carefully and look closely at all the details. Do you think these cartoons were making fun of Thomas Paine, honoring Paine, or both?

Wha Wants Me
(Published in London, December 26, 1792.)

Thomas Paine, full-length, standing, facing left, holding scroll "rights of man," surrounded by injustices and standing on labels, representing morals and justices, defending measures taken in revolutionary France and appealing to the English to overthrow their monarchy and organize a republic. *Library of Congress*

Tom Paine's Nightly Pest
(Published in London by H. Humphrey, December 10, 1792)

Tom Paine asleep, having a nightmare in which three faceless judges, illuminated by rays of light issuing from the scales of justice, unfurl scrolls listing charges and punishments; behind judges are gallows and stocks.
Library of Congress

A Good Constitution Sacrificed for a Fantastic Form
(or Fashion Before Ease)
Published in London by H. Humphrey, 1793.

Cartoon shows Britannia clasping trunk of a large oak, while Thomas Paine tugs with both hands at her stay laces, his foot on her posterior. From his coat pocket protrudes a pair of scissors and a tape inscribed: "Rights of Man." Behind him is a thatched cottage inscribed: "Thomas Pain, Staymaker from Thetford. Paris Modes, by express."

Common Sense

(Original Text)

by Thomas Paine

Addressed to the Inhabitants of America

January 10, 1776 (with additional material added February 14, 1776)

Introduction

PERHAPS the sentiments contained in the following pages, are not yet sufficiently fashionable to procure them general favor; a long habit of not thinking a thing wrong, gives it a superficial appearance of being right, and raises at first a formidable outcry in defence of custom. But tumult soon subsides. Time makes more converts than reason.

As a long and violent abuse of power is generally the means of calling the right of it in question, (and in matters too which might never have been thought of, had not the sufferers been aggravated into the inquiry,) and as the king of England hath undertaken in his own right, to support the parliament in what he calls theirs, and as the good people of this country are grievously oppressed by the combination, they have an undoubted privilege to inquire into the pretensions of both, and equally to reject the usurpations of either.

In the following sheets, the author hath studiously avoided every thing which is personal among ourselves. Compliments as well as censure to individuals make no part thereof. The wise and the worthy need not the triumph of a pamphlet; and those whose sentiments are injudicious or unfriendly, will cease of themselves, unless too much pains is bestowed upon their conversion.

The cause of America is, in a great measure, the cause of all mankind. Many circumstances have, and will arise, which are not local, but universal, and through which the principles of all lovers of mankind are affected, and in the event of which, their affections are interested. The laying a country desolate with fire and sword, declaring war against the natural rights of all mankind, and extirpating the defenders thereof from the face of the earth, is the concern of every man to whom nature hath given the power of feeling; of which class, regardless of party censure, is

THE AUTHOR.
Philadelphia, Feb. 14, 1776.

*   *   *

OF THE ORIGIN AND DESIGN OF GOVERNMENT IN GENERAL. WITH CONCISE REMARKS ON THE ENGLISH CONSTITUTION

SOME writers have so confounded society with government, as to leave little or no distinction between them; whereas they are not only different, but have different origins. Society is produced by our wants, and government by our wickedness; the former promotes our happiness positively by uniting our affections, the latter negatively by restraining our vices. The one encourages intercourse, the other creates distinctions. The first is a patron, the last a punisher.

Society in every state is a blessing, but government even in its best state is but a necessary evil in its worst state an intolerable one; for when we suffer, or are exposed to the same miseries by a government, which we might expect in a country without government, our calamities is heightened by reflecting that we furnish the means by which we suffer! Government, like dress, is the badge of lost innocence; the palaces of kings are built on the ruins of the bowers of paradise. For were the impulses of conscience clear, uniform, and irresistibly obeyed, man would need no other lawgiver; but that not being the case, he finds it necessary to surrender up a part of his property to furnish means

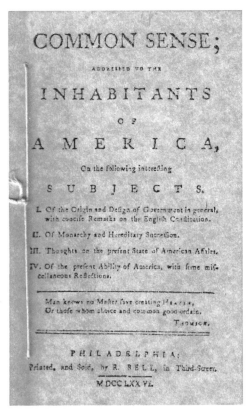

for the protection of the rest; and this he is induced to do by the same prudence which in every other case advises him out of two evils to choose the least. Wherefore, security being the true design and end of government, it unanswerably follows that whatever form thereof appears most likely to ensure it to us, with the least expense and greatest benefit, is preferable to all others.

In order to gain a clear and just idea of the design and end of government, let us suppose a small number of persons settled in some sequestered part of the earth, unconnected with the rest, they will then represent the first peopling of any country, or of the world. In this state of natural liberty, society will be their first thought. A thousand motives will excite them thereto, the strength of one man is so unequal to his wants, and his mind so unfitted for perpetual solitude, that he is soon obliged to seek assistance and relief of another, who in his turn requires the same. Four or five united would be able to raise a tolerable dwelling in the midst of a wilderness, but one man might labor out the common period of life without accomplishing any thing; when he had felled his timber he could not remove it, nor erect it after it was removed; hunger in the mean time would urge him from his work, and every different want call him a different way. Disease, nay even misfortune would be death, for though neither might be mortal, yet either would disable him from living, and reduce him to a state in which he might rather be said to perish than to die.

Thus necessity, like a gravitating power, would soon form our newly arrived emigrants into society, the reciprocal blessings of which, would supersede, and render the obligations of law and government unnecessary while they remained perfectly just to each other; but as nothing but heaven is impregnable to vice, it will unavoidably happen, that in proportion as they surmount the first difficulties of emigration, which bound them together in a common cause, they will begin to relax in their duty and attachment to each other; and this remissness, will point out the necessity, of establishing some form of government to supply the defect of moral virtue.

Some convenient tree will afford them a State-House, under the branches of which, the whole colony may assemble to deliberate on public matters. It is more than probable that their first laws will have the title only of Regulations, and be enforced by no other penalty than public disesteem. In this first parliament every man, by natural right will have a seat.

But as the colony increases, the public concerns will increase likewise, and the distance at which the members may be separated, will render it too inconvenient for all of them to meet on every occasion as at first, when their number was small, their habitations near, and the public concerns few and trifling. This will point out the convenience of their consenting to leave the legislative part to be managed by a select number chosen from the whole body, who are supposed to have the same concerns at stake which those have who appointed them, and who will act in the same manner as the whole body would act were they present. If the colony continue increasing, it will become necessary to augment the number of the representatives, and that the interest of every part of the colony may be attended to, it will be found best to divide the whole into convenient parts, each part sending its proper number; and that the elected might never form to themselves an interest separate from the electors, prudence will point out the propriety of having elections often; because as the elected might by that means return and mix again with the general body of the electors in a few months, their fidelity to the public will be secured by the prudent reflection of not making a rod for themselves. And as this frequent interchange will establish a common interest with every part of the community, they will mutually and naturally support each other, and on this (not on the unmeaning name of king) depends the strength of government, and the happiness of the governed.

Here then is the origin and rise of government; namely, a mode rendered necessary by the inability of moral virtue to govern the world; here too is the design and end of government, viz., freedom and security. And however our eyes may be dazzled with snow, or our ears deceived by sound; however prejudice may warp our wills, or interest darken our understanding, the simple voice of nature and of reason will say, it is right.

I draw my idea of the form of government from a principle in nature, which no art can overturn, viz., that the more simple any thing is, the less liable it is to be disordered, and the easier repaired when disordered; and with this maxim in view, I offer a few remarks on the so much boasted constitution of England. That it was noble for the dark and slavish times in which it was erected is granted. When the world was overrun with tyranny the least therefrom was a glorious rescue. But that it is imperfect, subject to convulsions, and incapable of producing what it seems to promise, is easily demonstrated.

Absolute governments (though the disgrace of human nature) have this advantage with them, that they are simple; if the people suffer, they know the head from which their suffering springs, know likewise the remedy, and are not bewildered by a variety of causes and cures. But the constitution of England is so exceedingly complex, that the nation may suffer for years together without being able to discover in which part the fault lies, some will say in one and some in another, and every political physician will advise a different medicine.

I know it is difficult to get over local or long standing prejudices, yet if we will suffer ourselves to examine the component parts of the English constitution, we shall find them to be the base remains of two ancient tyrannies, compounded with some new republican materials.

First.- The remains of monarchical tyranny in the person of the king. Secondly.- The remains of aristocratical tyranny in the persons of the peers. Thirdly.- The new republican materials, in the persons of the commons, on whose virtue depends the freedom of England.

The two first, by being hereditary, are independent of the people; wherefore in a constitutional sense they contribute nothing towards the freedom of the state.

To say that the constitution of England is a union of three powers reciprocally checking each other, is farcical, either the words have no meaning, or they are flat contradictions.

To say that the commons is a check upon the king, presupposes two things.

First.- That the king is not to be trusted without being looked after, or in other words, that a thirst for absolute power is the natural disease of monarchy. Secondly.- That the commons, by being appointed for that purpose, are either wiser or more worthy of confidence than the crown.

But as the same constitution which gives the commons a power to check the king by withholding the supplies, gives afterwards the king a power to check the commons, by empowering him to reject their other bills; it again supposes that the king is wiser than those whom it has already supposed to be wiser than him. A mere absurdity!

There is something exceedingly ridiculous in the composition of monarchy; it first excludes a man from the means of information, yet empowers him to act in cases where the highest judgment is required. The state of a king shuts him from the world, yet the business of a king requires him to know it thoroughly; wherefore the different parts, unnaturally opposing and destroying each other, prove the whole character to be absurd and useless.

Some writers have explained the English constitution thus; the king, say they, is one, the people another; the peers are an house in behalf of the king; the commons in behalf of the people; but this hath all the distinctions of an house divided against itself; and though the expressions be pleasantly arranged, yet when examined they appear idle and ambiguous; and it will always happen, that the nicest construction that words are capable of, when applied to the description of something which either cannot exist, or is too incomprehensible to be within the compass of description, will be words of sound only, and though they may amuse the ear, they cannot inform the mind, for this explanation includes a previous question, viz. How came the king by a power which the people are afraid to trust, and always obliged to check? Such a power could not be the gift of a wise people, neither can any power, which needs checking, be from God; yet the provision, which the constitution makes, supposes such a power to exist.

But the provision is unequal to the task; the means either cannot or will not accomplish the end, and the whole affair is a felo de se; for as the greater weight will always carry up the less, and as all the wheels of a machine are put in motion by one, it only remains to know which power in the constitution has the most weight, for that will govern; and though the others, or a part of them, may clog, or, as the phrase is, check the rapidity of its motion, yet so long as they cannot stop it, their endeavors will be ineffectual; the first moving power will at last have its way, and what it wants in speed is supplied by time.

That the crown is this overbearing part in the English constitution needs not be mentioned, and that it derives its whole consequence merely from being the giver of places pensions is self evident, wherefore, though we have and wise enough to shut and lock a door against absolute monarchy, we at the same time have been foolish enough to put the crown in possession of the key.

The prejudice of Englishmen, in favor of their own government by king, lords, and commons, arises as much or more from national pride than reason.

Individuals are undoubtedly safer in England than in some other countries, but the will of the king is as much the law of the land in Britain as in France, with this difference, that instead of proceeding directly from his mouth, it is handed to the people under the most formidable shape of an act of parliament. For the fate of Charles the First, hath only made kings more subtle not- more just.

Wherefore, laying aside all national pride and prejudice in favor of modes and forms, the plain truth is, that it is wholly owing to the constitution of the people, and not to the constitution of the government that the crown is not as oppressive in England as in Turkey.

An inquiry into the constitutional errors in the English form of government is at this time highly necessary; for as we are never in a proper condition of doing justice to others, while we continue under the influence of some leading partiality, so neither are we capable of doing it to ourselves while we remain fettered by any obstinate prejudice. And as a man, who is attached to a prostitute, is unfitted to choose or judge of a wife, so any prepossession in favor of a rotten constitution of government will disable us from discerning a good one.

OF MONARCHY AND HEREDITARY SUCCESSION

MANKIND being originally equals in the order of creation, the equality could only be destroyed by some subsequent circumstance; the distinctions of rich, and poor, may in a great measure be accounted for, and that without having recourse to the harsh, ill-sounding names of oppression and avarice. Oppression is often the consequence, but seldom or never the means of riches; and though avarice will preserve a man from being necessitously poor, it generally makes him too timorous to be wealthy. But there is another and greater distinction for which no truly natural or religious reason can be assigned, and that is, the distinction of men into KINGS and SUBJECTS. Male and female are the distinctions of nature, good and bad the distinctions of heaven; but how a race of men came into the world so exalted above the rest, and distinguished like some new species, is worth enquiring into, and whether they are the means of happiness or of misery to mankind.

In the early ages of the world, according to the scripture chronology, there were no kings; the consequence of which was there were no wars; it is the pride of kings which throw mankind into confusion. Holland without a king hath enjoyed more peace for this last century than any of the monarchial governments in Europe. Antiquity favors the same remark; for the quiet and rural lives of the first patriarchs hath a happy something in them, which vanishes away when we come to the history of Jewish royalty.

Government by kings was first introduced into the world by the Heathens, from whom the children of Israel copied the custom. It was the most prosperous invention the Devil ever set on foot for the promotion of idolatry. The Heathens paid divine honors to their deceased kings, and the Christian world hath improved on the plan by doing the same to their living ones. How impious is the title of sacred majesty applied to a worm, who in the midst of his splendor is crumbling into dust!

As the exalting one man so greatly above the rest cannot be justified on the equal rights of nature, so neither can it be defended on the authority of scripture; for the will of the Almighty, as declared by Gideon and the prophet Samuel, expressly disapproves of government by kings. All anti-monarchial parts of scripture have been very smoothly glossed over in monarchial governments, but they undoubtedly merit the attention of countries which have their governments yet to form. Render unto Caesar the things which are Caesar's is the scriptural doctrine of courts, yet it is no support of monarchial government, for the Jews at that time were without a king, and in a state of vassalage to the Romans.

Near three thousand years passed away from the Mosaic account of the creation, till the Jews under a national delusion requested a king. Till then their form of government (except in extraordinary cases, where the Almighty interposed) was a kind of republic administered by a judge and the elders of the tribes. Kings they had none, and it was held sinful to acknowledge any being under that title but the Lords of Hosts. And when a man seriously reflects on the idolatrous homage which is paid to the persons of kings he need not wonder, that the Almighty, ever jealous of his honor, should disapprove of a form of government which so impiously invades the prerogative of heaven.

Monarchy is ranked in scripture as one of the sins of the Jews, for which a curse in reserve is denounced against them. The history of that transaction is worth attending to.

The children of Israel being oppressed by the Midianites, Gideon marched against them with a small army, and victory, through the divine interposition, decided in his favor. The Jews elate with success, and attributing it to the generalship of Gideon, proposed making him a king, saying, Rule thou over us, thou and thy son and thy son's son. Here was temptation in its fullest extent; not a kingdom only, but an hereditary one, but Gideon in the piety of his soul replied, I will not rule over you, neither shall my son rule over you, THE LORD SHALL RULE OVER YOU. Words need not be more explicit; Gideon doth not decline the honor but denieth their right to give it; neither doth be compliment them with invented declarations of his thanks, but in the positive stile of a prophet charges them with disaffection to their proper sovereign, the King of Heaven.

About one hundred and thirty years after this, they fell again into the same error. The hankering which the Jews had for the idolatrous customs of the Heathens, is something exceedingly unaccountable; but so it was, that laying hold of the misconduct of Samuel's two sons, who were entrusted with some secular concerns, they came in an abrupt and clamorous manner to Samuel, saying, Behold thou art old and thy sons walk not in thy ways, now make us a king to judge us like all the other nations. And here we cannot but observe that their motives were bad, viz., that they might be like unto other nations, i.e., the Heathen, whereas their true glory laid in being as much unlike them as possible. But the thing displeased Samuel when they said, give us a king to judge us; and

Samuel prayed unto the Lord, and the Lord said unto Samuel, Hearken unto the voice of the people in all that they say unto thee, for they have not rejected thee, but they have rejected me, THEN I SHOULD NOT REIGN OVER THEM.

According to all the works which have done since the day; wherewith they brought them up out of Egypt, even unto this day; wherewith they have forsaken me and served other Gods; so do they also unto thee. Now therefore hearken unto their voice, howbeit, protest solemnly unto them and show them the manner of the king that shall reign over them, i.e., not of any particular king, but the general manner of the kings of the earth, whom Israel was so eagerly copying after. And notwithstanding the great distance of time and difference of manners, the character is still in fashion. And Samuel told all the words of the Lord unto the people, that asked of him a king. And he said, This shall be the manner of the king that shall reign over you; he will take your sons and appoint them for himself for his chariots, and to be his horsemen, and some shall run before his chariots (this description agrees with the present mode of impressing men) and he will appoint him captains over thousands and captains over fifties, and will set them to ear his ground and to read his harvest, and to make his instruments of war, and instruments of his chariots; and he will take your daughters to be confectionaries and to be cooks and to be bakers (this describes the expense and luxury as well as the oppression of kings) and he will take your fields and your olive yards, even the best of them, and give them to his servants; and he will take the tenth of your seed, and of your vineyards, and give them to his officers and to his servants (by which we see that bribery, corruption, and favoritism are the standing vices of kings) and he will take the tenth of your men servants, and your maid servants, and your goodliest young men and your asses, and put them to his work; and he will take the tenth of your sheep, and ye shall be his servants, and ye shall cry out in that day because of your king which ye shall have chosen, AND THE LORD WILL NOT HEAR YOU IN THAT DAY. This accounts for the continuation of monarchy; neither do the characters of the few good kings which have lived since, either sanctify the title, or blot out the sinfulness of the origin; the high encomium given of David takes no notice of him officially as a king, but only as a man after God's own heart. Nevertheless the People refused to obey the voice of Samuel, and they said, Nay, but we will have a king over us, that we may be like all the nations, and that our king may judge us, and go out before us and fight our battles. Samuel continued to reason with them, but to no purpose; he set before them their ingratitude, but all would not avail; and seeing them fully bent on their folly, he cried out, I will call unto the Lord, and he shall sent thunder and rain (which then was a punishment, being the time of wheat harvest) that ye may perceive and see that your wickedness is great which ye have done in the sight of the Lord, IN ASKING YOU A KING. So Samuel called unto the Lord, and the Lord sent thunder and rain that day, and all the people greatly feared the Lord and Samuel And all the people said unto Samuel, Pray for thy servants unto the Lord thy God that we die not, for WE HAVE ADDED UNTO OUR SINS THIS EVIL, TO ASK A KING. These portions of scripture are direct and positive. They admit of no equivocal construction. That the Almighty hath here entered his protest against monarchial government is true, or the scripture is false. And a man hath good reason to believe that there is as much of kingcraft, as priestcraft in withholding the scripture from the public in Popish countries. For monarchy in every instance is the Popery of government.

To the evil of monarchy we have added that of hereditary succession; and as the first is a degradation and lessening of ourselves, so the second, claimed as a matter of right, is an insult and an imposition on posterity. For all men being originally equals, no one by birth could have a right to set up his own family in perpetual preference to all others for ever, and though himself might deserve some decent degree of honors of his contemporaries, yet his descendants might be far too unworthy to inherit them. One of the strongest natural proofs of the folly of hereditary right in kings, is, that nature disapproves it, otherwise she would not so frequently turn it into ridicule by giving mankind an ass for a lion.

Secondly, as no man at first could possess any other public honors than were bestowed upon him, so the givers of those honors could have no power to give away the right of posterity, and though they might say, "We choose you for our head," they could not, without manifest injustice to their children, say, "that your children and your children's children shall reign over ours for ever." Because such an unwise, unjust, unnatural compact might (perhaps) in the next succession put them under the government of a rogue or a fool. Most wise men, in their private sentiments, have ever treated hereditary right with contempt; yet it is one of those evils, which when once established is not easily removed; many submit from fear, others from superstition, and the more powerful part shares with the king the plunder of the rest.

This is supposing the present race of kings in the world to have had an honorable origin; whereas it is more than probable, that could we take off the dark covering of antiquity, and trace them to their first rise, that we should find the first of them nothing better than the principal ruffian of some restless gang, whose savage manners of preeminence in subtlety obtained him the title of chief among plunderers; and who by increasing in power, and extending his depredations, overawed the quiet and defenseless to purchase their safety by frequent contributions. Yet his electors could have no idea of giving hereditary right to his descendants, because such a perpetual exclusion of themselves was incompatible with the free and unrestrained principles they professed to live by. Wherefore, hereditary succession in the early ages of monarchy could not take place as a matter of claim, but as something casual or complemental; but as few or no records were extant in those days, and traditionary history stuffed with fables, it was very easy, after the lapse of a few generations, to trump up some superstitious tale, conveniently timed, Mahomet like, to cram hereditary right down the throats of the vulgar. Perhaps the disorders which threatened, or seemed to threaten on the decease of a leader and the choice of a new one (for elections among ruffians could not be very orderly) induced many at first to favor hereditary pretensions; by which means it happened, as it hath happened since, that what at first was submitted to as a convenience, was afterwards claimed as a right.

England, since the conquest, hath known some few good monarchs, but groaned beneath a much larger number of bad ones, yet no man in his senses can say that their claim under William the Conqueror is a very honorable one. A French bastard landing with an armed banditti, and establishing himself king of England against the consent of the natives, is in plain terms a very paltry rascally original. It certainly hath no divinity in it. However, it is needless to spend much time in exposing the folly of hereditary right, if there are any so weak as to believe it, let them promiscuously worship the ass and lion, and welcome. I shall neither copy their humility, nor disturb their devotion.

Yet I should be glad to ask how they suppose kings came at first? The question admits but of three answers, viz., either by lot, by election, or by usurpation. If the first king was taken by lot, it establishes a precedent for the next, which excludes hereditary succession. Saul was by lot, yet the succession was not hereditary, neither does it appear from that transaction there was any intention it ever should. If the first king of any country was by election, that likewise establishes a precedent for the next; for to say, that the right of all future generations is taken away, by the act of the first electors, in their choice not only of a king, but of a family of kings for ever, hath no parallel in or out of scripture but the doctrine of original sin, which supposes the free will of all men lost in Adam; and from such comparison, and it will admit of no other, hereditary succession can derive no glory. For as in Adam all sinned, and as in the first electors all men obeyed; as in the one all mankind were subjected to Satan, and in the other to Sovereignty; as our innocence was lost in the first, and our authority in the last; and as both disable us from reassuming some former state and privilege, it unanswerably follows that original sin and hereditary succession are parallels. Dishonorable rank! Inglorious connection! Yet the most subtle sophist cannot produce a juster simile.

As to usurpation, no man will be so hardy as to defend it; and that William the Conqueror was an usurper is a fact not to be contradicted. The plain truth is, that the antiquity of English monarchy will not bear looking into.

But it is not so much the absurdity as the evil of hereditary succession which concerns mankind. Did it ensure a race of good and wise men it would have the seal of divine authority, but as it opens a door to the foolish, the wicked; and the improper, it hath in it the nature of oppression. Men who look upon themselves born to reign, and others to obey, soon grow insolent; selected from the rest of mankind their minds are early poisoned by importance; and the world they act in differs so materially from the world at large, that they have but little opportunity of knowing its true interests, and when they succeed to the government are frequently the most ignorant and unfit of any throughout the dominions.

Another evil which attends hereditary succession is, that the throne is subject to be possessed by a minor at any age; all which time the regency, acting under the cover of a king, have every opportunity and inducement to betray their trust. The same national misfortune happens, when a king worn out with age and infirmity, enters the last stage of human weakness. In both these cases the public becomes a prey to every miscreant, who can tamper successfully with the follies either of age or infancy.

The most plausible plea, which hath ever been offered in favor of hereditary succession, is, that it preserves a nation from civil wars; and were this true, it would be weighty; whereas, it is the most barefaced falsity ever imposed upon mankind. The whole history of England disowns the fact. Thirty kings and two minors have reigned in that distracted kingdom since the conquest, in which time there have been (including the Revolution) no less than eight civil wars and nineteen rebellions. Wherefore instead of making for peace, it makes against it, and destroys the very foundation it seems to stand on.

The contest for monarchy and succession, between the houses of York and Lancaster, laid England in a scene of blood for many years. Twelve pitched battles, besides skirmishes and sieges, were fought between Henry and Edward. Twice was Henry prisoner to Edward, who in his turn was prisoner to Henry. And so uncertain is the fate of war and the temper of a nation, when nothing but personal matters are the ground of a quarrel, that Henry was taken in triumph from a prison to a palace, and Edward obliged to fly from a palace to a foreign land; yet, as sudden transitions of temper are seldom lasting, Henry in his turn was driven from the throne, and Edward recalled to succeed him. The parliament always following the strongest side.

This contest began in the reign of Henry the Sixth, and was not entirely extinguished till Henry the Seventh, in whom the families were united. Including a period of 67 years, viz., from 1422 to 1489.

In short, monarchy and succession have laid (not this or that kingdom only) but the world in blood and ashes. 'Tis a form of government which the word of God bears testimony against, and blood will attend it.

If we inquire into the business of a king, we shall find that (in some countries they have none) and after sauntering away their lives without pleasure to themselves or advantage to the nation, withdraw from the scene, and leave their successors to tread the same idle round. In absolute monarchies the whole weight of business civil and military, lies on the king; the children of Israel in their request for a king, urged this plea "that he may judge us, and go out before us and fight our battles." But in countries where he is neither a judge nor a general, as in England, a man would be puzzled to know what is his business.

The nearer any government approaches to a republic, the less business there is for a king. It is somewhat difficult to find a proper name for the government of England. Sir William Meredith calls it a republic; but in its present state it is unworthy of the name, because the corrupt influence If the crown, by having all the places in its disposal, hath so effectually swallowed up the power, and eaten out the virtue of the house of commons (the republican part in the constitution) that the government of England is nearly as monarchical as that of France or

Spain. Men fall out with names without understanding them. For it is the republican and not the monarchical part of the constitution of England which Englishmen glory in, viz., the liberty of choosing a house of commons from out of their own body- and it is easy to see that when the republican virtue fails, slavery ensues. My is the constitution of England sickly, but because monarchy hath poisoned the republic, the crown hath engrossed the commons?

In England a king hath little more to do than to make war and give away places; which in plain terms, is to impoverish the nation and set it together by the ears. A pretty business indeed for a man to be allowed eight hundred thousand sterling a year for, and worshipped into the bargain! Of more worth is one honest man to society, and in the sight of God, than all the crowned ruffians that ever lived.

THOUGHTS OF THE PRESENT STATE OF AMERICAN AFFAIRS

IN the following pages I offer nothing more than simple facts, plain arguments, and common sense; and have no other preliminaries to settle with the reader, than that he will divest himself of prejudice and prepossession, and suffer his reason and his feelings to determine for themselves; that he will put on, or rather that he will not put off the true character of a man, and generously enlarge his views beyond the present day.

Volumes have been written on the subject of the struggle between England and America. Men of all ranks have embarked in the controversy, from different motives, and with various designs; but all have been ineffectual, and the period of debate is closed. Arms, as the last resource, decide the contest; the appeal was the choice of the king, and the continent hath accepted the challenge.

It hath been reported of the late Mr. Pelham (who tho' an able minister was not without his faults) that on his being attacked in the house of commons, on the score, that his measures were only of a temporary kind, replied, "they will fast my time." Should a thought so fatal and unmanly possess the colonies in the present contest, the name of ancestors will be remembered by future generations with detestation.

The sun never shined on a cause of greater worth. 'Tis not the affair of a city, a country, a province, or a kingdom, but of a continent- of at least one eighth part of the habitable globe. 'Tis not the concern of a day, a year, or an age; posterity are virtually involved in the contest, and will be more or less affected, even to the end of time, by the proceedings now. Now is the seed time of continental union, faith and honor. The least fracture now will be like a name engraved with the point of a pin on the tender rind of a young oak; The wound will enlarge with the tree, and posterity read it in full grown characters.

By referring the matter from argument to arms, a new area for politics is struck; a new method of thinking hath arisen. All plans, proposals, &c. prior to the nineteenth of April, i.e., to the commencement of hostilities, are like the almanacs of the last year; which, though proper then, are superseded and useless now. Whatever was advanced by the advocates on either side of the question then, terminated in one and the same point, viz., a union with Great Britain; the only difference between the parties was the method of effecting it; the one proposing force, the other friendship; but it hath so far happened that the first hath failed, and the second hath withdrawn her influence.

As much hath been said of the advantages of reconciliation, which, like an agreeable dream, hath passed away and left us as we were, it is but right, that we should examine the contrary side of the argument, and inquire into some of the many material injuries which these colonies sustain, and always will sustain, by being connected with, and dependant on Great Britain. To examine that connection and dependance, on the principles of nature and common sense, to see what we have to trust to, if separated, and what we are to expect, if dependant.

I have heard it asserted by some, that as America hath flourished under her former connection with Great Britain, that the same connection is necessary towards her future happiness, and will always have the same effect. Nothing can be more fallacious than this kind of argument. We may as well assert, that because a child has thrived upon milk, that it is never to have meat; or that the first twenty years of our lives is to become a precedent for the next twenty. But even this is admitting more than is true, for I answer roundly, that America would have flourished as much, and probably much more, had no European power had any thing to do with her. The commerce by which she hath enriched herself are the necessaries of life, and will always have a market while eating is the custom of Europe.

But she has protected us, say some. That she hath engrossed us is true, and defended the continent at our expense as well as her own is admitted, and she would have defended Turkey from the same motive, viz., the sake of trade and dominion.

Alas! we have been long led away by ancient prejudices and made large sacrifices to superstition. We have boasted the protection of Great Britain, without considering, that her motive was interest not attachment; that she did not protect us from our enemies on our account, but from her enemies on her own account, from those who had no quarrel with us on any other account, and who will always be our enemies on the same account. Let Britain wave her pretensions to the continent, or the continent throw off the dependance, and we should be at peace with France and Spain were they at war with Britain. The miseries of Hanover last war, ought to warn us against connections.

It hath lately been asserted in parliament, that the colonies have no relation to each other but through the parent country, i.e., that Pennsylvania and the Jerseys, and so on for the rest, are sister colonies by the way of England; this is certainly a very roundabout way of proving relation ship, but it is the nearest and only true way of proving enemyship, if I may so call it. France and Spain never were, nor perhaps ever will be our enemies as Americans, but as our being the subjects of Great Britain.

*B*ut Britain is the parent country, say some. Then the more shame upon her conduct. Even brutes do not devour their young; nor savages make war upon their families; wherefore the assertion, if true, turns to her reproach; but it happens not to be true, or only partly so, and the phrase parent or mother country hath been jesuitically adopted by the king and his parasites, with a low papistical design of gaining an unfair bias on the credulous weakness of our minds. Europe, and not England, is the parent country of America. This new world hath been the asylum for the persecuted lovers off civil and religious liberty from every Part of Europe. Hither have they fled, not from the tender embraces of the mother, but from the cruelty of the monster; and it is so far true of England, that the same tyranny which drove the first emigrants from home pursues their descendants still.

*I*n this extensive quarter of the globe, we forget the narrow limits of three hundred and sixty miles (the extent of England) and carry our friendship on a larger scale; we claim brotherhood with every European Christian, and triumph in the generosity of the sentiment.

*I*t is pleasant to observe by what regular gradations we surmount the force of local prejudice, as we enlarge our acquaintance with the world. A man born in any town in England divided into parishes, will naturally associate most with his fellow parishioners (because their interests in many cases will be common) and distinguish him by the name of neighbor; if he meet him but a few miles from home, he drops the narrow idea of a street, and salutes him by the name of townsman; if he travels out of the county, and meet him in any other, he forgets the minor divisions of street and town, and calls him countryman; i.e., countyman; but if in their foreign excursions they should associate in France or any other part of Europe, their local remembrance would be enlarged into that of Englishmen. And by a just parity of reasoning, all Europeans meeting in America, or any other quarter of the globe, are countrymen; for England, Holland, Germany, or Sweden, when compared with the whole, stand in the same places on the larger scale, which the divisions of street, town, and county do on the smaller ones; distinctions too limited for continental minds. Not one third of the inhabitants, even of this province, are of English descent. Wherefore, I reprobate the phrase of parent or mother country applied to England only, as being false, selfish, narrow and ungenerous.

*B*ut admitting that we were all of English descent, what does it amount to? Nothing. Britain, being now an open enemy, extinguishes every other name and title: And to say that reconciliation is our duty, is truly farcical. The first king of England, of the present line (William the Conqueror) was a Frenchman, and half the peers of England are descendants from the same country; wherefore by the same method of reasoning, England ought to be governed by France.

*M*uch hath been said of the united strength of Britain and the colonies, that in conjunction they might bid defiance to the world. But this is mere presumption; the fate of war is uncertain, neither do the expressions mean anything; for this continent would never suffer itself to be drained of inhabitants to support the British arms in either Asia, Africa, or Europe.

Besides, what have we to do with setting the world at defiance? Our plan is commerce, and that, well attended to, will secure us the peace and friendship of all Europe; because it is the interest of all Europe to have America a free port. Her trade will always be a protection, and her barrenness of gold and silver secure her from invaders.

I challenge the warmest advocate for reconciliation, to show, a single advantage that this continent can reap, by being connected with Great Britain. I repeat the challenge, not a single advantage is derived. Our corn will fetch its price in any market in Europe, and our imported goods must be paid for buy them where we will.

But the injuries and disadvantages we sustain by that connection, are without number; and our duty to mankind I at large, as well as to ourselves, instruct us to renounce the alliance: Because, any submission to, or dependance on Great Britain, tends directly to involve this continent in European wars and quarrels; and sets us at variance with nations, who would otherwise seek our friendship, and against whom, we have neither anger nor complaint. As Europe is our market for trade, we ought to form no partial connection with any part of it. It is the true interest of America to steer clear of European contentions, which she never can do, while by her dependance on Britain, she is made the make-weight in the scale of British politics.

Europe is too thickly planted with kingdoms to be long at peace, and whenever a war breaks out between England and any foreign power, the trade of America goes to ruin, because of her connection with Britain. The next war may not turn out like the Past, and should it not, the advocates for reconciliation now will be wishing for separation then, because, neutrality in that case, would be a safer convoy than a man of war. Every thing that is right or natural pleads for separation. The blood of the slain, the weeping voice of nature cries, 'tis time to part. Even the distance at which the Almighty hath placed England and America, is a strong and natural proof, that the authority of the one, over the other, was never the design of Heaven. The time likewise at which the continent was discovered, adds weight to the argument, and the manner in which it was peopled increases the force of it. The reformation was preceded by the discovery of America, as if the Almighty graciously meant to open a sanctuary to the persecuted in future years, when home should afford neither friendship nor safety.

The authority of Great Britain over this continent, is a form of government, which sooner or later must have an end: And a serious mind can draw no true pleasure by looking forward, under the painful and positive conviction, that what he calls "the present constitution" is merely temporary. As parents, we can have no joy, knowing that this government is not sufficiently lasting to ensure any thing which we may bequeath to posterity: And by a plain method of argument, as we are running the next generation into debt, we ought to do the work of it, otherwise we use them meanly and pitifully. In order to discover the line of our duty rightly, we should take our children in our hand, and fix our station a few years farther into life; that eminence will present a prospect, which a few present fears and prejudices conceal from our sight.

Though I would carefully avoid giving unnecessary offence, yet I am inclined to believe, that all those who espouse the doctrine of reconciliation, may be included within the following descriptions:

Interested men, who are not to be trusted; weak men who cannot see; prejudiced men who will not see; and a certain set of moderate men, who think better of the European world than it deserves; and this last class by an ill-judged deliberation, will be the cause of more calamities to this continent than all the other three.

It is the good fortune of many to live distant from the scene of sorrow; the evil is not sufficiently brought to their doors to make them feel the precariousness with which all American property is possessed. But let our imaginations transport us for a few moments to Boston, that seat of wretchedness will teach us wisdom, and instruct us for ever to renounce a power in whom we can have no trust. The inhabitants of that unfortunate city, who but a few months ago were in ease and affluence, have now no other alternative than to stay and starve, or turn out to beg. Endangered by the fire of their friends if they continue within the city, and plundered by the soldiery if they leave it. In their present condition they are prisoners without the hope of redemption, and in a general attack for their relief, they would be exposed to the fury of both armies.

Men of passive tempers look somewhat lightly over the offenses of Britain, and, still hoping for the best, are apt to call out, Come we shall be friends again for all this. But examine the passions and feelings of mankind. Bring the doctrine of reconciliation to the touchstone of nature, and then tell me, whether you can hereafter love, honor, and faithfully serve the power that hath carried fire and sword into your land? If you cannot do all these, then are you only deceiving yourselves, and by your delay bringing ruin upon posterity. Your future connection with Britain, whom you can neither love nor honor, will be forced and unnatural, and being formed only on the plan of present convenience, will in a little time fall into a relapse more wretched than the first. But if you say, you can still pass the violations over, then I ask, Hath your house been burnt? Hath you property been destroyed before your face? Are your wife and children destitute of a bed to lie on, or bread to live on? Have you lost a parent or a child by their hands, and yourself the ruined and wretched survivor? If you have not, then are you not a judge of those who have. But if you have, and can still shake hands with the murderers, then are you unworthy the name of husband, father, friend, or lover, and whatever may be your rank or title in life, you have the heart of a coward, and the spirit of a sycophant.

This is not inflaming or exaggerating matters, but trying them by those feelings and affections which nature justifies, and without which, we should be incapable of discharging the social duties of life, or enjoying the felicities of it. I mean not to exhibit horror for the purpose of provoking revenge, but to awaken us from fatal and unmanly slumbers, that we may pursue determinately some fixed object. It is not in the power of Britain or of Europe to conquer America, if she do not conquer herself by delay and timidity. The present winter is worth an age if rightly employed, but if lost or neglected, the whole continent will partake of the misfortune; and there is no punishment which that man will not deserve, be he who, or what, or where he will, that may be the means of sacrificing a season so precious and useful.

It is repugnant to reason, to the universal order of things, to all examples from the former ages, to suppose, that this continent can longer remain subject to any external power. The most sanguine in Britain does not think so. The utmost stretch of human wisdom cannot, at this time compass a plan short of separation, which can promise the continent even a year's security. Reconciliation is was a fallacious dream. Nature hath deserted the connection, and Art cannot supply her place. For, as Milton wisely expresses, "never can true reconcilement grow where wounds of deadly hate have pierced so deep."

Every quiet method for peace hath been ineffectual. Our prayers have been rejected with disdain; and only tended to convince us, that nothing flatters vanity, or confirms obstinacy in kings more than repeated petitioning- and nothing hath contributed more than that very measure to make the kings of Europe absolute: Witness Denmark and Sweden. Wherefore since nothing but blows will do, for God's sake, let us come to a final separation, and not leave the next generation to be cutting throats, under the violated unmeaning names of parent and child.

To say, they will never attempt it again is idle and visionary, we thought so at the repeal of the stamp act, yet a year or two undeceived us; as well me we may suppose that nations, which have been once defeated, will never renew the quarrel.

As to government matters, it is not in the powers of Britain to do this continent justice: The business of it will soon be too weighty, and intricate, to be managed with any tolerable degree of convenience, by a power, so distant from us, and so very ignorant of us; for if they cannot conquer us, they cannot govern us. To be always running three or four thousand miles with a tale or a petition, waiting four or five months for an answer, which when obtained requires five or six more to explain it in, will in a few years be looked upon as folly and childishness- there was a time when it was proper, and there is a proper time for it to cease.

Small islands not capable of protecting themselves, are the proper objects for kingdoms to take under their care; but there is something very absurd, in supposing a continent to be perpetually governed by an island. In no instance hath nature made the satellite larger than its primary planet, and as England and America, with respect to each Other, reverses the common order of nature, it is evident they belong to different systems: England to Europe- America to itself.

*J*am not induced by motives of pride, party, or resentment to espouse the doctrine of separation and independence; I am clearly, positively, and conscientiously persuaded that it is the true interest of this continent to be so; that every thing short of that is mere patchwork, that it can afford no lasting felicity,- that it is leaving the sword to our children, and shrinking back at a time, when, a little more, a little farther, would have rendered this continent the glory of the earth.

*A*s Britain hath not manifested the least inclination towards a compromise, we may be assured that no terms can be obtained worthy the acceptance of the continent, or any ways equal to the expense of blood and treasure we have been already put to.

*T*he object contended for, ought always to bear some just proportion to the expense. The removal of the North, or the whole detestable junto, is a matter unworthy the millions we have expended. A temporary stoppage of trade, was an inconvenience, which would have sufficiently balanced the repeal of all the acts complained of, had such repeals been obtained; but if the whole continent must take up arms, if every man must be a soldier, it is scarcely worth our while to fight against a contemptible ministry only. Dearly, dearly, do we pay for the repeal of the acts, if that is all we fight for; for in a just estimation, it is as great a folly to pay a Bunker Hill price for law, as for land. As I have always considered the independency of this continent, as an event, which sooner or later must arrive, so from the late rapid progress of the continent to maturity, the event could not be far off. Wherefore, on the breaking out of hostilities, it was not worth the while to have disputed a matter, which time would have finally redressed, unless we meant to be in earnest; otherwise, it is like wasting an estate of a suit at law, to regulate the trespasses of a tenant, whose lease is just expiring. No man was a warmer wisher for reconciliation than myself, before the fatal nineteenth of April, 1775 (Massacre at Lexington), but the moment the event of that day was made known, I rejected the hardened, sullen tempered Pharaoh of England for ever; and disdain the wretch, that with the pretended title of Father of his people, can unfeelingly hear of their slaughter, and composedly sleep with their blood upon his soul.

*B*ut admitting that matters were now made up, what would be the event? I answer, the ruin of the continent. And that for several reasons:

*F*irst. The powers of governing still remaining in the hands of the king, he will have a negative over the whole legislation of this continent. And as he hath shown himself such an inveterate enemy to liberty, and discovered such a thirst for arbitrary power, is he, or is he not, a proper man to say to these colonies, "You shall make no laws but what I please?" And is there any inhabitants in America so ignorant, as not to know, that according to what is called the present constitution, that this continent can make no laws but what the king gives leave to? and is there any man so unwise, as not to see, that (considering what has happened) he will suffer no Law to be made here, but such as suit his purpose? We may be as effectually enslaved by the want of laws in America, as by submitting to laws made for us in England. After matters are make up (as it is called) can there be any doubt but the whole power of the crown will be exerted, to keep this continent as low and humble as possible? Instead of going forward we shall go backward, or be perpetually quarrelling or ridiculously petitioning. We are already greater than the king wishes us to be, and will he not hereafter endeavor to make us less? To bring the matter to one point. Is the power who is jealous of our prosperity, a proper power to govern us? Whoever says No to this question is an independent, for independency means no more, than, whether we shall make our own laws, or whether the king, the greatest enemy this continent hath, or can have, shall tell us, "there shall be now laws but such as I like."

But the king you will say has a negative in England; the people there can make no laws without his consent. in point of right and good order, there is something very ridiculous, that a youth of twenty-one (which hath often happened) shall say to several millions of people, older and wiser than himself, I forbid this or that act of yours to be law. But in this place I decline this sort of reply, though I will never cease to expose the absurdity of it, and only answer, that England being the king's residence, and America not so, make quite another case. The king's negative here is ten times more dangerous and fatal than it can be in England, for there he will scarcely refuse his consent to a bill for putting England into as strong a state of defence as possible, and in America he would never suffer such a bill to be passed.

America is only a secondary object in the system of British politics-England consults the good of this country, no farther than it answers her own purpose. Wherefore, her own interest leads her to suppress the growth of ours in every case which doth not promote her advantage, or in the least interfere with it. A pretty state we should soon be in under such a second-hand government, considering what has happened! Men do not change from enemies to friends by the alteration of a name; and in order to show that reconciliation now is a dangerous doctrine, I affirm, that it would be policy in the kingdom at this time, to repeal the acts for the sake of reinstating himself in the government of the provinces; in order, that he may accomplish by craft and subtlety, in the long run, wha he cannot do by force ans violence in the short one. Reconciliation and ruin are nearly related.

Secondly. That as even the best terms, which we can expect to obtain, can amount to no more than a temporary expedient, or a kind of government by guardianship, which can last no longer than till the colonies come of age, so the general face and state of things, in the interim, will be unsettled and unpromising. Emigrants of property will not choose to come to a country whose form of government hangs but by a thread, and who is every day tottering on the brink of commotion and disturbance; and numbers of the present inhabitant would lay hold of the interval, to dispose of their effects, and quit the continent.

But the most powerful of all arguments, is, that nothing but independence, i.e., a continental form of government, can keep the peace of the continent and preserve it inviolate from civil wars. I dread the event of a reconciliation with

Britain now, as it is more than probable, that it will be followed by a revolt somewhere or other, the consequences of which may be far more fatal than all the malice of Britain.

Thousands are already ruined by British barbarity; (thousands more will probably suffer the same fate.) Those men have other feelings than us who have nothing suffered. All they now possess is liberty, what they before enjoyed is sacrificed to its service, and having nothing more to lose, they disdain submission. Besides, the general temper of the colonies, towards a British government, will be like that of a youth, who is nearly out of his time, they will care very little about her. And a government which cannot preserve the peace, is no government at all, and in that case we pay our money for nothing; and pray what is it that Britain can do, whose power will be wholly on paper, should a civil tumult break out the very day after reconciliation? I have heard some men say, many of whom I believe spoke without thinking, that they dreaded independence, fearing that it would produce civil wars. It is but seldom that our first thoughts are truly correct, and that is the case here; for there are ten times more to dread from a patched up connection than from independence. I make the sufferers case my own, and I protest, that were I driven from house and home, my property destroyed, and my circumstances ruined, that as man, sensible of injuries, I could never relish the doctrine of reconciliation, or consider myself bound thereby.

The colonies have manifested such a spirit of good order and obedience to continental government, as is sufficient to make every reasonable person easy and happy on that head. No man can assign the least pretence for his fears, on any other grounds, that such as are truly childish and ridiculous, viz., that one colony will be striving for superiority over another.

Where there are no distinctions there can be no superiority, perfect equality affords no temptation. The republics of Europe are all (and we may say always) in peace. Holland and Switzerland are without wars, foreign or domestic; monarchical governments, it is true, are never long at rest: the crown itself is a temptation to enterprising ruffians at home; and that degree of pride and insolence ever attendant on regal authority swells into a rupture with foreign powers, in instances where a republican government, by being formed on more natural principles, would negotiate the mistake.

If there is any true cause of fear respecting independence it is because no plan is yet laid down. Men do not see their way out; wherefore, as an opening into that business I offer the following hints; at the same time modestly affirming, that I have no other opinion of them myself, than that they may be the means of giving rise to something better. Could the straggling thoughts of individuals be collected, they would frequently form materials for wise and able men to improve to useful matter.

Let the assemblies be annual, with a President only. The representation more equal. Their business wholly domestic, and subject to the authority of a continental congress.

$\mathcal{L}$et each colony be divided into six, eight, or ten, convenient districts, each district to send a proper number of delegates to congress, so that each colony send at least thirty. The whole number in congress will be at least three hundred ninety. Each congress to sit. . . . and to choose a president by the following method. When the delegates are met, let a colony be taken from the whole thirteen colonies by lot, after which let the whole congress choose (by ballot) a president from out of the delegates of that province. I the next Congress, let a colony be taken by lot from twelve only, omitting that colony from which the president was taken in the former congress, and so proceeding on till the whole thirteen shall have had their proper rotation. And in order that nothing may pass into a law but what is satisfactorily just, not less than three fifths of the congress to be called a majority. He that will promote discord, under a government so equally formed as this, would join Lucifer in his revolt.

$\mathcal{B}$ut as there is a peculiar delicacy, from whom, or in what manner, this business must first arise, and as it seems most agreeable and consistent, that it should come from some intermediate body between the governed and the governors, that is between the Congress and the people, let a Continental Conference be held, in the following manner, and for the following purpose:

$\mathcal{A}$ committee of twenty-six members of Congress, viz., two for each colony. Two members for each house of assembly, or provincial convention; and five representatives of the people at large, to be chosen in the capital city or town of each province, for, and in behalf of the whole province, by as many qualified voters as shall think proper to attend from all parts of the province for that purpose; or, if more convenient, the representatives may be chosen in two or three of the most populous parts thereof. In this conference, thus assembled, will be united, the two grand principles of business, knowledge and power. The members of Congress, Assemblies, or Conventions, by having had experience in national concerns, will be able and useful counsellors, and the whole, being empowered by the people will have a truly legal authority.

$\mathcal{T}$he conferring members being met, let their business be to frame a Continental Charter, or Charter of the United Colonies; (answering to what is called the Magna Charta of England) fixing the number and manner of choosing members of Congress, members of Assembly, with their date of sitting, and drawing the line of business and jurisdiction between them: always remembering, that our strength is continental, not provincial: Securing freedom and property to all men, and above all things the free exercise of religion, according to the dictates of conscience; with such other matter as is necessary for a charter to contain. Immediately after which, the said conference to dissolve, and the bodies which shall be chosen conformable to the said charter, to be the legislators and governors of this continent for the time being: Whose peace and happiness, may God preserve, Amen.

$\mathcal{S}$hould any body of men be hereafter delegated for this or some similar purpose, I offer them the following extracts from that wise observer on governments Dragonetti. "The science" says he, "of the politician consists in fixing the true point of happiness and freedom. Those men would deserve the gratitude of ages, who should discover a mode of government that contained the greatest sum of individual happiness, with the least national expense."- Dragonetti on Virtue and Rewards.

But where says some is the king of America? I'll tell you Friend, he reigns above, and doth not make havoc of mankind like the Royal of Britain. Yet that we may not appear to be defective even in earthly honors, let a day be solemnly set apart for proclaiming the charter; let it be brought forth placed on the divine law, the word of God; let a crown be placed thereon, by which the world may know, that so far as we approve of monarchy, that in America the law is king. For as in absolute governments the king is law, so in free countries the law ought to be king; and there ought to be no other. But lest any ill use should afterwards arise, let the crown at the conclusion of the ceremony be demolished, and scattered among the people whose right it is.

A government of our own is our natural right: And when a man seriously reflects on the precariousness of human affairs, he will become convinced, that it is in finitely wiser and safer, to form a constitution of our own in a cool deliberate manner, while we have it in our power, than to trust such an interesting event to time and chance. If we omit it now, some Massenello* may hereafter arise, who laying hold of popular disquietudes, may collect together the desperate and the discontented, and by assuming to themselves the powers of government, may sweep away the liberties of the continent like a deluge. Should the government of America return again into the hands of Britain, the tottering situation of things, will be a temptation for some desperate adventurer to try his fortune; and in such a case, what relief can Britain give? Ere she could hear the news the fatal business might be done, and ourselves suffering like the wretched Britons under the oppression of the Conqueror. Ye that oppose independence now, ye know not what ye do; ye are opening a door to eternal tyranny, by keeping vacant the seat of government.

*Thomas Anello, otherwise Massenello, a fisherman of Naples, who after spiriting up his countrymen in the public market place, against the oppression of the Spaniards, to whom the place was then subject, prompted them to revolt, and in the space of a day became king.)

There are thousands and tens of thousands; who would think it glorious to expel from the continent, that barbarous and hellish power, which hath stirred up the Indians and Negroes to destroy us; the cruelty hath a double guilt, it is dealing brutally by us, and treacherously by them. To talk of friendship with those in whom our reason forbids us to have faith, and our affections, (wounded through a thousand pores) instruct us to detest, is madness and folly. Every day wears out the little remains of kindred between us and them, and can there be any reason to hope, that as the relationship expires, the affection will increase, or that we shall agree better, when we have ten times more and greater concerns to quarrel over than ever?

Ye that tell us of harmony and reconciliation, can ye restore to us the time that is past? Can ye give to prostitution its former innocence? Neither can ye reconcile Britain and America. The last cord now is broken, the people of England are presenting addresses against us. There are injuries which nature cannot forgive; she would cease to be nature if she did. As well can the lover forgive the ravisher of his mistress, as the continent forgive the murders of Britain. The Almighty hath implanted in us these inextinguishable feelings for good and wise purposes. They are the guardians of his image in our hearts. They distinguish us from the herd of common animals. The social compact would dissolve, and justice be extirpated the earth, of have only a casual existence were we callous to the touches of affection. The robber and the murderer, would often escape unpunished, did not the injuries which our tempers sustain, provoke us into justice.

O ye that love mankind! Ye that dare oppose, not only the tyranny, but the tyrant, stand forth! Every spot of the old world is overrun with oppression. Freedom hath been hunted round the globe. Asia, and Africa, have long expelled her. Europe regards her like a stranger, and England hath given her warning to depart. O! receive the fugitive, and prepare in time an asylum for mankind.

OF THE PRESENT ABILITY OF AMERICA, WITH SOME MISCELLANEOUS REFLECTIONS

I have never met with a man, either in England or America, who hath not confessed his opinion, that a separation between the countries, would take place one time or other. And there is no instance in which we have shown less judgment, than in endeavoring to describe, what we call, the ripeness or fitness of the Continent for independence.

As all men allow the measure, and vary only in their opinion of the time, let us, in order to remove mistakes, take a general survey of things and endeavor if possible, to find out the very time. But we need not go far, the inquiry ceases at once, for the time hath found us. The general concurrence, the glorious union of all things prove the fact.

It is not in numbers but in unity, that our great strength lies; yet our present numbers are sufficient to repel the force of all the world. The Continent hath, at this time, the largest body of armed and disciplined men of any power under Heaven; and is just arrived at that pitch of strength, in which no single colony is able to support itself, and the whole, who united can accomplish the matter, and either more, or, less than this, might be fatal in its effects. Our land force is already sufficient, and as to naval affairs, we cannot be insensible, that Britain would never suffer an American man of war to be built while the continent remained in her hands. Wherefore we should be no forwarder an hundred years hence in that branch, than we are now; but the truth is, we should be less so, because the timber of the country is every day diminishing, and that which will remain at last, will be far off and difficult to procure.

Were the continent crowded with inhabitants, her sufferings under the present circumstances would be intolerable. The more sea port towns we had, the more should we have both to defend and to loose. Our present numbers are so happily proportioned to our wants, that no man need be idle. The diminution of trade affords an army, and the necessities of an army create a new trade. Debts we have none; and whatever we may contract on this account will serve as a glorious memento of our virtue. Can we but leave posterity with a settled form of government, an independent constitution of its own, the purchase at any price will be cheap. But to expend millions for the sake of getting a few we acts repealed, and routing the present ministry only, is unworthy the charge, and is using posterity with the utmost cruelty; because it is leaving them the great work to do, and a debt upon their backs, from which they derive no advantage. Such a thought is unworthy a man of honor, and is the true characteristic of a narrow heart and a peddling politician.

The debt we may contract doth not deserve our regard if the work be but accomplished. No nation ought to be without a debt. A national debt is a national bond; and when it bears no interest, is in no case a grievance. Britain is oppressed with a debt of upwards of one hundred and forty millions sterling, for which she pays upwards of four millions interest. And as a compensation for her debt, she has a large navy; America is without a debt, and without a navy; yet for the twentieth part of the English national debt, could have a navy as large again. The navy of England is not worth more than three millions and a half sterling.

The first and second editions of this pamphlet were published without the following calculations, which are now given as a proof that the above estimation of the navy is a just one. (See Entick's naval history, intro. page 56.)

The charge of building a ship of each rate, and furnishing her with masts, yards, sails and rigging, together with a proportion of eight months boatswain's and carpenter's sea-stores, as calculated by Mr. Burchett, Secretary to the navy, is as follows:

For a ship of 100 guns	£35,553
90	£29,886
80	£23,638
70	£17,785
60	£14,197
50	£10,606
40	£7,558

30	£5,846
20	£3,710

And from hence it is easy to sum up the value, or cost rather, of the whole British navy, which in the year 1757, when it was as its greatest glory consisted of the following ships and guns:

Ships	Guns	Cost of one	Cost of all
6	100	£35,533	£213,318
12	90	£29,886	£358,632
12	80	£23,638	£283,656
43	70	£17,785	£746,755
35	60	£14,197	£496,895
40	50	£10,606	£424,240
45	40	£7,758	£344,110
58	20	£3,710	£215,180
85 Sloops, bombs, and fireships, one another		£2,000	£170,000
Cost			£3,266,786
Remains for guns			£229,214
Total			£3,500,000

No country on the globe is so happily situated, so internally capable of raising a fleet as America. Tar, timber, iron, and cordage are her natural produce. We need go abroad for nothing. Whereas the Dutch, who make large profits by hiring out their ships of war to the Spaniards and Portuguese, are obliged to import most of the materials they use. We ought to view the building a fleet as an article of commerce, it being the natural manufactory of this country. It is the best money we can lay out. A navy when finished is worth more than it cost. And is that nice point in national policy, in which commerce and protection are united. Let us build; if we want them not, we can sell; and by that means replace our paper currency with ready gold and silver.

In point of manning a fleet, people in general run into great errors; it is not necessary that one-fourth part should be sailors. The privateer Terrible, Captain Death, stood the hottest engagement of any ship last war, yet had not twenty sailors on board, though her complement of men was upwards of two hundred. A few able and social sailors will soon instruct a sufficient number of active landsmen in the common work of a ship. Wherefore, we never can be more capable to begin on maritime matters than now, while our timber is standing, our fisheries blocked up, and our sailors and shipwrights out of employ. Men of war of seventy and eighty guns were built forty years ago in New England, and why not the same now? Ship building is America's greatest pride, and in which, she will in time excel the whole world. The great empires of the east are mostly inland, and consequently excluded from the possibility of rivalling her. Africa is in a state of barbarism; and no power in Europe, hath either such an extent or coast, or such an internal supply of materials. Where nature hath given the one, she has withheld the other; to America only hath she been liberal of both. The vast empire of Russia is almost shut out from the sea; wherefore, her boundless forests, her tar, iron, and cordage are only articles of commerce.

In point of safety, ought we to be without a fleet? We are not the little people now, which we were sixty years ago; at that time we might have trusted our property in the streets, or fields rather; and slept securely without locks or bolts to our doors or windows. The case now is altered, and our methods of defence ought to improve with our increase of property. A common pirate, twelve months ago, might have come up the Delaware, and laid the city of Philadelphia under instant contribution, for what sum he pleased; and the same might have happened to other places. Nay, any daring fellow, in a brig of fourteen or sixteen guns, might have robbed the whole Continent, and carried off half a million of money. These are circumstances which demand our attention, and point out the necessity of naval protection.

Some, perhaps, will say, that after we have made it up with Britain, she will protect us. Can we be so unwise as to mean, that she shall keep a navy in our harbors for that purpose? Common sense will tell us, that the power which hath endeavored to subdue us, is of all others the most improper to defend us. Conquest may be effected under the pretence of friendship; and ourselves, after a long and brave resistance, be at last cheated into slavery. And if her ships are not to be admitted into our harbors, I would ask, how is she to protect us? A navy three or four thousand miles off can be of little use, and on sudden emergencies, none at all. Wherefore, if we must hereafter protect ourselves, why not do it for ourselves? Why do it for another.

The English list of ships of war is long and formidable, but not a tenth part of them are at any one time fit for service, numbers of them not in being; yet their names are pompously continued in the list, if only a plank be left of the ship: and not a fifth part, of such as are fit for service, can be spared on any one station at one time. The East, and West Indies, Mediterranean, Africa, and other parts over which Britain extends her claim, make large demands upon her navy. From a mixture of prejudice and inattention, we have contracted a false notion respecting the navy of England, and have talked as if we should have the whole of it to encounter at once, and for that reason, supposed that we must have one as large; which not being instantly practicable, have been made use of by a set of disguised tories to discourage our beginning thereon. Nothing can be farther from truth than this; for if America had only a twentieth part of the naval force of Britain, she would be by far an over match for her; because, as we neither have, nor claim any foreign dominion, our whole force would be employed on our own coast, where we should, in the long run, have two to one the advantage of those who had three or four thousand miles to sail over, before they could attack us, and the same distance to return in order to refit and recruit. And although Britain by her fleet, hath a check over our trade to Europe, we have as large a one over her trade to the West Indies, which, by laying in the neighborhood of the Continent, is entirely at its mercy.

Some method might be fallen on to keep up a naval force in time of peace, if we should not judge it necessary to support a constant navy. If premiums were to be given to merchants, to build and employ in their service, ships mounted with twenty, thirty, forty, or fifty guns, (the premiums to be in proportion to the loss of bulk to the merchants) fifty or sixty of those ships, with a few guard ships on constant duty, would keep up a sufficient navy, and that without burdening ourselves with the evil so loudly complained of in England, of suffering their fleet, in time of peace to lie rotting in the docks. To unite the sinews of commerce and defence is sound policy; for when our strength and our riches, play into each other's hand, we need fear no external enemy.

In almost every article of defence we abound. Hemp flourishes even to rankness, so that we need not want cordage. Our iron is superior to that of other countries. Our small arms equal to any in the world. Cannon we can cast at pleasure. Saltpetre and gunpowder we are every day producing. Our knowledge is hourly improving. Resolution is our inherent character, and courage hath never yet forsaken us. Wherefore, what is it that we want? Why is it that we hesitate? From Britain we can expect nothing but ruin. If she is once admitted to the government of America again, this Continent will not be worth living in. Jealousies will be always arising; insurrections will be constantly happening; and who will go forth to quell them? Who will venture his life to reduce his own countrymen to a foreign obedience? The difference between Pennsylvania and Connecticut, respecting some unlocated lands, shows the insignificance of a British government, and fully proves, that nothing but Continental authority can regulate Continental matters.

Another reason why the present time is preferable to all others, is, that the fewer our numbers are, the more land there is yet unoccupied, which instead of being lavished by the king on his worthless dependents, may be hereafter applied, not only to the discharge of the present debt, but to the constant support of government. No nation under heaven hath such an advantage as this.

The infant state of the Colonies, as it is called, so far from being against, is an argument in favor of independence. We are sufficiently numerous, and were we more so, we might be less united. It is a matter worthy of observation, that the more a country is peopled, the smaller their armies are. In military numbers, the ancients far exceeded the moderns: and the reason is evident, for trade being the consequence of population, men become too much absorbed thereby to attend to anything else. Commerce diminishes the spirit, both of patriotism and military defence. And history sufficiently informs us, that the bravest achievements were always accomplished in the non-age of a nation. With the increase of commerce England hath lost its spirit. The city of London, notwithstanding its numbers, submits to continued insults with the patience of a coward. The more men have to lose, the less willing are they to venture. The rich are in general slaves to fear, and submit to courtly power with the trembling duplicity of a spaniel.

Youth is the seed-time of good habits, as well in nations as in individuals. It might be difficult, if not impossible, to form the Continent into one government half a century hence. The vast variety of interests, occasioned by an increase of trade and population, would create confusion. Colony would be against colony. Each being able might scorn each other's assistance: and while the proud and foolish gloried in their little distinctions, the wise would lament that the union had not been formed before. Wherefore, the present time is the true time for establishing it. The intimacy which is contracted in infancy, and the friendship which is formed in misfortune, are, of all others, the most lasting and unalterable. Our present union is marked with both these characters: we are young, and we have been distressed; but our concord hath withstood our troubles, and fixes a memorable area for posterity to glory in.

The present time, likewise, is that peculiar time, which never happens to a nation but once, viz., the time of forming itself into a government. Most nations have let slip the opportunity, and by that means have been compelled to receive laws from their conquerors, instead of making laws for themselves. First, they had a king, and then a form of government; whereas, the articles or charter of government, should be formed first, and men delegated to execute them afterwards: but from the errors of other nations, let us learn wisdom, and lay hold of the present opportunity- to begin government at the right end.

When William the Conqueror subdued England he gave them law at the point of the sword; and until we consent that the seat of government in America, be legally and authoritatively occupied, we shall be in danger of having it filled by some fortunate ruffian, who may treat us in the same manner, and then, where will be our freedom? where our property?

As to religion, I hold it to be the indispensable duty of all government, to protect all conscientious professors thereof, and I know of no other business which government hath to do therewith. Let a man throw aside that narrowness of soul, that selfishness of principle, which the niggards of all professions are so unwilling to part with, and he will be at once delivered of his fears on that head. Suspicion is the companion of mean souls, and the bane of all good society. For myself I fully and conscientiously believe, that it is the will of the Almighty, that there should be diversity of religious opinions among us: It affords a larger field for our Christian kindness. Were we all of one way of thinking, our religious dispositions would want matter for probation; and on this liberal principle, I look on the various denominations among us, to be like children of the same family, differing only, in what is called their Christian names.

Earlier in this work, I threw out a few thoughts on the propriety of a Continental Charter, (for I only presume to offer hints, not plans) and in this place, I take the liberty of rementioning the subject, by observing, that a charter is to be understood as a bond of solemn obligation, which the whole enters into, to support the right of every separate part, whether of religion, personal freedom, or property, A firm bargain and a right reckoning make long friends.

In a former page I likewise mentioned the necessity of a large and equal representation; and there is no political matter which more deserves our attention. A small number of electors, or a small number of representatives, are equally dangerous. But if the number of the representatives be not only small, but unequal, the danger is increased. As an instance of this, I mention the following; when the Associators petition was before the House of Assembly of Pennsylvania; twenty-eight members only were present, all the Bucks County members, being eight, voted against it, and had seven of the Chester members done the same, this whole province had been governed by two counties only, and this danger it is always exposed to. The unwarrantable stretch likewise, which that house made in their last sitting, to gain an undue authority over the delegates of that province, ought to warn the people at large, how they trust power out of their own hands. A set of instructions for the Delegates were put together, which in point of sense and business would have dishonored a school-boy, and after being approved by a few, a very few without doors, were carried into the house, and there passed in behalf of the whole colony; whereas, did the whole colony know, with what ill-will that House hath entered on some necessary public measures, they would not hesitate a moment to think them unworthy of such a trust.

Immediate necessity makes many things convenient, which if continued would grow into oppressions. Expedience and right are different things. When the calamities of America required a consultation, there was no method so ready, or at that time so proper, as to appoint persons from the several Houses of

Assembly for that purpose and the wisdom with which they have proceeded hath preserved this continent from ruin. But as it is more than probable that we shall never be without a Congress, every well-wisher to good order, must own, that the mode for choosing members of that body, deserves consideration. And I put it as a question to those, who make a study of mankind, whether representation and election is not too great a power for one and the same body of men to possess? When we are planning for posterity, we ought to remember that virtue is not hereditary.

It is from our enemies that we often gain excellent maxims, and are frequently surprised into reason by their mistakes. Mr. Cornwall (one of the Lords of the Treasury) treated the petition of the New York Assembly with contempt, because that House, he said, consisted but of twenty-six members, which trifling number, he argued, could not with decency be put for the whole. We thank him for his involuntary honesty.*

Those who would fully understand of what great consequence a large and equal representation is to a state, should read Burgh's political Disquisitions.

To conclude: However strange it may appear to some, or however unwilling they may be to think so, matters not, but many strong and striking reasons may be given, to show, that nothing can settle our affairs so expeditiously as an open and determined declaration for independence. Some of which are:

First. It is the custom of nations, when any two are at war, for some other powers, not engaged in the quarrel, to step in as mediators, and bring about the preliminaries of a peace: but while America calls herself the subject of Great Britain, no power, however well disposed she may be, can offer her mediation. Wherefore, in our present state we may quarrel on for ever.

Secondly. It is unreasonable to suppose, that France or Spain will give us any kind of assistance, if we mean only to make use of that assistance for the purpose of repairing the breach, and strengthening the connection between Britain and America; because, those powers would be sufferers by the consequences.

Thirdly. While we profess ourselves the subjects of Britain, we must, in the eye of foreign nations, be considered as rebels. The precedent is somewhat dangerous to their peace, for men to be in arms under the name of subjects; we on the spot, can solve the paradox: but to unite resistance and subjection, requires an idea much too refined for common understanding.

Fourthly. Were a manifesto to be published, and despatched to foreign courts, setting forth the miseries we have endured, and the peaceable methods we have ineffectually used for redress; declaring, at the same time, that not being able, any longer to live happily or safely under the cruel disposition of the British court, we had been driven to the necessity of breaking off all connection with her; at the same time assuring all such courts of our peaceable disposition towards them, and of our desire of entering into trade with them. Such a memorial would produce more good effects to this Continent, than if a ship were freighted with petitions to Britain.

Under our present denomination of British subjects we can neither be received nor heard abroad: The custom of all courts is against us, and will be so, until, by an independence, we take rank with other nations.

These proceedings may at first appear strange and difficult; but, like all other steps which we have already passed over, will in a little time become familiar and agreeable; and, until an independence is declared, the continent will feel itself like a man who continues putting off some unpleasant business from day to day, yet knows it must be done, hates to set about it, wishes it over, and is continually haunted with the thoughts of its necessity.

Mr. Paine added the following text to the original Common Sense approximately a month after the original came out on January 10, 1776.

In this additional material, Paine talks about the King's Proclamation (see page 98) that arrived in the colonies at the same time that Common Sense was published. Paine believes this was a very fortunate coincidence.

APPENDIX

SINCE the publication of the first edition of this pamphlet, or rather, on the same day on which it came out, the king's speech made its appearance in this city. Had the spirit of prophecy directed the birth of this production, it could not have brought it forth, at a more seasonable juncture, or a more necessary time. The bloody-mindedness of the one, show the necessity of pursuing the doctrine of the other. Men read by way of revenge. And the speech instead of terrifying, prepared a way for the manly principles of independence.

Ceremony, and even, silence, from whatever motive they may arise, have a hurtful tendency, when they give the least degree of countenance to base and wicked performances; wherefore, if this maxim be admitted, it naturally follows, that the king's speech, as being a piece of finished villainy, deserved, and still deserves, a general execration both by the congress and the people. Yet as the domestic tranquility of a nation, depends greatly on the chastity of what may properly be called national manners, it is often better, to pass some things over in silent disdain, than to make use of such new methods of dislike, as might introduce the least innovation, on that guardian of our peace and safety. And perhaps, it is chiefly owing to this prudent delicacy, that the king's speech, hath not before now, suffered a public execution. The speech if it may be called one, is nothing better than a wilful audacious libel against the truth, the common good, and the existence of mankind; and is a formal and pompous method of offering up human sacrifices to the pride of tyrants. But this general massacre of mankind, is one of the privileges, and the certain consequences of kings; for as nature knows them not, they know not her, and although they are beings of our own creating, they know not us, and are become the gods of their creators. The speech hath one good quality, which is, that it is not calculated to deceive, neither can we, even if we would, be deceived by it. Brutality and tyranny appear on the face of it. It leaves us at no loss: And every line convinces, even in the moment of reading, that He, who hunts the woods for prey, the naked and untutored Indian, is less a savage than the king of Britain.

Sir John Dalrymple, the putative father of a whining jesuitical piece, fallaciously called, The address of the people of ENGLAND to the inhabitants of America, hath, perhaps from a vain supposition, that the people here were to be frightened at the pomp and description of a king, given, (though very unwisely on his part) the real character of the present one: "But," says this writer, "if you are inclined to pay compliments to an administration, which we do not complain of," (meaning the Marquis of Rockingham's at the repeal of the Stamp Act) "it is very unfair in you to withhold them from that prince, by whose NOD ALONE they were permitted to do anything." This is toryism with a witness! Here is idolatry even without a mask: And he who can calmly hear, and digest such doctrine, hath forfeited his claim to rationality an apostate from the order of manhood; and ought to be considered- as one, who hath, not only given up the proper dignity of a man, but sunk himself beneath the rank of animals, and contemptibly crawl through the world like a worm.

However, it matters very little now, what the king of England either says or does; he hath wickedly broken through every moral and human obligation, trampled nature and conscience beneath his feet; and by a steady and constitutional spirit of insolence and cruelty, procured for himself an universal hatred. It is now the interest of America to provide for herself. She hath already a large and young family, whom it is more her duty to take care of, than to be granting away her property, to support a power who is become a reproach to the names of men and Christians. Ye, whose office it is to watch over the morals of a nation, of whatsoever sect or denomination ye are of, as well as ye, who are more immediately the guardians of the public liberty, if ye wish to preserve your native country uncontaminated by European corruption, ye must in secret wish a separation But leaving the moral part to private reflection, I shall chiefly confine my farther remarks to the following heads:

First. That it is the interest of America to be separated from Britain. Secondly. Which is the easiest and most practicable plan, reconciliation or independence? with some occasional remarks.

In support of the first, I could, if I judged it proper, produce the opinion of some of the ablest and most experienced men on this continent; and whose sentiments, on that head, are not yet publicly known. It is in reality a self-evident position: For no nation in a state of foreign dependance, limited in its commerce, and cramped and fettered in its legislative powers, can ever arrive at any material eminence. America doth not yet know what opulence is; and although the progress which she hath made stands unparalleled in the history of other nations, it is but childhood, compared with what she would be capable of arriving at, had she, as she ought to have, the legislative powers in her own hands. England is, at this time, proudly coveting what would do her no good, were she to accomplish it; and the Continent hesitating on a matter, which will be her final ruin if neglected. It is the commerce and not the conquest of America, by which England is to be benefited, and that would in a great measure continue, were the countries as independent of each other as France and Spain; because in many articles, neither can go to a better market. But it is the independence of this country on Britain or any other which is now the main and only object worthy of contention, and which, like all other truths discovered by necessity, will appear clearer and stronger every day.

First. Because it will come to that one time or other. Secondly. Because the longer it is delayed the harder it will be to accomplish.

I have frequently amused myself both in public and private companies, with silently remarking the spacious errors of those who speak without reflecting. And among the many which I have heard, the following seems the most general, viz., that had this rupture happened forty or fifty years hence, instead of now, the Continent would have been more able to have shaken off the dependance. To which I reply, that our military ability at this time, arises from the experience gained in the last war, and which in forty or fifty years time, would have been totally extinct. The Continent, would not, by that time, have had a General, or even a military officer left; and we, or those who may succeed us, would have been as ignorant of martial matters as the ancient Indians: And this single position, closely attended to, will unanswerably prove, that the present time is preferable to all others: The argument turns thus- at the conclusion of the last war, we had experience, but wanted numbers; and forty or fifty years hence, we should have numbers, without experience; wherefore, the proper point of time, must be some particular point between the two extremes, in which a sufficiency of the former remains, and a proper increase of the latter is obtained: And that point of time is the present time.

The reader will pardon this digression, as it does not properly come under the head I first set out with, and to which I again return by the following position, viz.:

Should affairs be patched up with Britain, and she to remain the governing and sovereign power of America, (which as matters are now circumstanced, is giving up the point entirely) we shall deprive ourselves of the very means of sinking the debt we have or may contract. The value of the back lands which some of the provinces are clandestinely deprived of, by the unjust extension of the limits of Canada, valued only at five pounds sterling per hundred acres, amount to upwards of twenty-five millions, Pennsylvania currency; and the quit-rents at one penny sterling per acre, to two millions yearly.

It is by the sale of those lands that the debt may be sunk, without burden to any, and the quit-rent reserved thereon, will always lessen, and in time, will wholly support the yearly expense of government. It matters not how long the debt is in paying, so that the lands when sold be applied to the discharge of it, and for the execution of which, the Congress for the time being, will be the continental trustees.

I proceed now to the second head, viz. Which is the earliest and most practicable plan, reconciliation or independence? with some occasional remarks.

He who takes nature for his guide is not easily beaten out of his argument, and on that ground, I answer generally- That INDEPENDENCE being a SINGLE SIMPLE LINE, contained within ourselves; and reconciliation, a matter exceedingly perplexed and complicated, and in which, a treacherous capricious court is to interfere, gives the answer without a doubt.

The present state of America is truly alarming to every man who is capable of reflection. Without law, without government, without any other mode of power than what is founded on, and granted by courtesy. Held together by an unexampled concurrence of sentiment, which is nevertheless subject to change, and which every secret enemy is endeavoring to dissolve. Our present condition, is, legislation without law; wisdom without a plan; a constitution without a name; and, what is strangely astonishing, perfect Independence contending for dependance. The instance is without a precedent; the case never existed before; and who can tell what may be the event? The property of no man is secure in the present unbraced system of things. The mind of the multitude is left at random, and feeling no fixed object before them, they pursue such as fancy or opinion starts. Nothing is criminal; there is no such thing as treason; wherefore, every one thinks himself at liberty to act as he pleases. The tories dared not to have assembled offensively, had they known that their lives, by that act were forfeited to the laws of the state. A line of distinction should be drawn, between English soldiers taken in battle, and inhabitants of America taken in arms. The first are prisoners, but the latter traitors. The one forfeits his liberty the other his head.

Notwithstanding our wisdom, there is a visible feebleness in some of our proceedings which gives encouragement to dissensions. The Continental Belt is too loosely buckled. And if something is not done in time, it will be too late to do any thing, and we shall fall into a state, in which, neither reconciliation nor independence will be practicable. The king and his worthless adherents are got at their old game of dividing the continent, and there are not wanting among us printers, who will be busy spreading specious falsehoods. The artful and hypocritical letter which appeared a few months ago in two of the New York papers, and likewise in two others, is an evidence that there are men who want either judgment or honesty. It is easy getting into holes and corners and talking of reconciliation: But do such men seriously consider, how difficult the task is, and how dangerous it may prove, should the Continent divide thereon. Do they take within their view, all the various orders of men whose situation and circumstances, as well as their own, are to be considered therein. Do they put themselves in the place of the sufferer whose all is already gone, and of the soldier, who hath quitted all for the defence of his country. If their ill judged moderation be suited to their own private situations only, regardless of others, the event will convince them, that "they are reckoning without their Host."

But us, says some, on the footing we were in the year 1763: To which I answer, the request is not now in the power of Britain to comply with, neither will she propose it; but if it were, and even should be granted, I ask, as a reasonable question, By what means is such a corrupt and faithless court to be kept to its engagements? Another parliament, nay, even the present, may hereafter repeal the obligation, on the pretence of its being violently obtained, or unwisely granted; and in that case, Where is our redress? No going to law with nations; cannon are the barristers of crowns; and the sword, not of justice, but of war, decides the suit. To be on the footing of 1763, it is not sufficient, that the laws only be put on the same state, but, that our circumstances, likewise, be put on the same state; our burnt and destroyed towns repaired or built up, our private losses made good, our public debts (contracted for defence) discharged; otherwise, we shall be millions worse than we were at that enviable period. Such a request had it been complied with a year ago, would have won the heart and soul of the continent- but now it is too late, "the Rubicon is passed."

Besides the taking up arms, merely to enforce the repeal of a pecuniary law, seems as unwarrantable by the divine law, and as repugnant to human feelings, as the taking up arms to enforce obedience thereto. The object, on either side, doth not justify the ways and means; for the lives of men are too valuable to be cast away on such trifles. It is the violence which is done and threatened to our persons; the destruction of our property by an armed force; the invasion of our country by fire and sword, which conscientiously qualifies the use of arms: And the instant, in which such a mode of defence became necessary, all subjection to Britain ought to have ceased; and the independency of America should have been considered, as dating its area from, and published by, the first musket that was fired against her. This line is a line of consistency; neither drawn by caprice, nor extended by ambition; but produced by a chain of events, of which the colonies were not the authors.

I shall conclude these remarks, with the following timely and well intended hints, We ought to reflect, that there are three different ways by which an independency may hereafter be effected; and that one of those three, will one day or other, be the fate of America, viz. By the legal voice of the people in congress; by a military power; or by a mob: It may not always happen that our soldiers are citizens, and the multitude a body of reasonable men; virtue, as I have already remarked, is not hereditary, neither is it perpetual. Should an independency be brought about by the first of those means, we have every opportunity and every encouragement before us, to form the noblest, purest constitution on the face of the earth. We have it in our power to begin the world over again. A situation, similar to the present, hath not happened since the days of Noah until now. The birthday of a new world is at hand, and a race of men perhaps as numerous as all Europe contains, are to receive their portion of freedom from the event of a few months. The reflection is awful- and in this point of view, how trifling, how ridiculous, do the little, paltry cavillings, of a few weak or interested men appear, when weighed against the business of a world.

Should we neglect the present favorable and inviting period, and an independence be hereafter effected by any other means, we must charge the consequence to ourselves, or to those rather, whose narrow and prejudiced souls, are habitually opposing the measure, without either inquiring or reflecting. There are reasons to be given in support of Independence, which men should rather privately think of, than be publicly told of. We ought not now to be debating whether we shall be independent or not, but, anxious to accomplish it on a firm, secure, and honorable basis, and uneasy rather that it is not yet began upon. Every day convinces us of its necessity. Even the tories (if such beings yet remain among us) should, of all men, be the most solicitous to promote it; for, as the appointment of committees at first, protected them from popular rage, so, a wise and well established form of government, will be the only certain means of continuing it securely to them. Wherefore, if they have not virtue enough to be Whigs, they ought to have prudence enough to wish for independence.

In short, independence is the only bond that can tie and keep us together. We shall then see our object, and our ears will be legally shut against the schemes of an intriguing, as well as a cruel enemy. We shall then too, be on a proper footing, to treat with Britain; for there is reason to conclude, that the pride of that court, will be less hurt by treating with the American states for terms of peace, than with those, whom she denominates, "rebellious subjects," for terms of accommodation. It is our delaying it that encourages her to hope for conquest, and our backwardness tends only to prolong the war. As we have, without any good effect therefrom, withheld our trade to obtain a redress of our grievances, let us now try the alternative, by independently redressing them ourselves, and then offering to open the trade. The mercantile and reasonable part of England will be still with us; because, peace with trade, is preferable to war without it. And if this offer be not accepted, other courts may be applied to.

On these grounds I rest the matter. And as no offer hath yet been made to refute the doctrine contained in the former editions of this pamphlet, it is a negative proof, that either the doctrine cannot be refuted, or, that the party in favor of it are too numerous to be opposed. Wherefore, instead of gazing at each other with suspicious or doubtful curiosity, let each of us, hold out to his neighbor the hearty hand of friendship, and unite in drawing a line, which, like an act of oblivion, shall bury in forgetfulness every former dissention. Let the names of Whig and Tory be extinct; and let none other be heard among us, than those of a good citizen, an open and resolute friend, and a virtuous supporter of the RIGHTS of MANKIND and of the FREE AND INDEPENDENT STATES OF AMERICA.

Answer Key

British Invasion of New York (page 143)

1: 283,940 (Pounds Sterling)
2: 169,696
3: 119,544
4: 148,400
5: 721,580
6:    240
7: 24,000
8:    400
9:     15
10: 1,500

National Park Webquest (page 148)

1. Fort Necessity 1754: George Washington

2. Old Fort Western: A week or more

3. Dorchester Heights: 59 Cannon

4. Paul Revere's House: Samuel Adams and John Hancock

5. Old North Church: The King

6. Thomas Paine Monument: "that try men's souls."

7. King George III: Contribution to the Civil List (civil government costs such as salaries for judges and ambassadors) and the expenses of the Royal Household.

8. Paul Revere's Midnight Ride: Menotomy

~ Glossary ~

Absolute: A ruler or authority completely free from rules or laws.

Absolute monarchy: A government in which one person (a king, for example), has total power.

Allegiance: Loyalty.

Assemblies: A group of people who gather to discuss and create laws.

Asylum: A place of safety.

Avarice: Greedy: a never-ending desire for wealth.

Banned: Something that is not allowed.

Barbarity: Act of cruelty.

Boatswain: A naval officer in charge of maintaining the hull (body) of a ship.

Brute: To act cruelly, or use your power to harm others.

Chaos: Total confusion.

Check: A way to limit or stop parts of a government from becoming all-powerful.

Civil: The general public, their activities, needs, etc.

Civil War: A war between conflicting groups of citizens of the same country for control of the government.

Commerce: Buying and selling goods on a large scale (often using ships to transport the goods).

Compromise: Settlement of differences, each giving up something to reach peace.

Constitution: The founding document setting forth the general principles and laws of a country.

Contempt: Total disrespect or lack of respect; disobedience.

Cordage: Rope.

Crown: Royalty and the power that flows from it.

Descendants: Children, offspring.

Disciplined: Orderly, trained, and developed.

Domestic: Affairs within your own country.

Dominate: To have control and/or power over something or someone.

Dominions: One of the self-governing nations within Great Britain's influence.

Emigrant: People who leave their country to move to another.

Enormous: Very large.

Envy: Ill feelings and resentment at seeing the success of another.

Farcical: Laughable, absurd, ludicrous.

Fleet: A number of warships under a single or unified command.

Habitable: Something that can be lived in.

Hemp: A tough fibrous plant used to make rope.

Hesitate: To delay before acting or deciding.

Hostilities: Conflict, open acts of warfare, opposition or resistance.

Import: To bring items into a country from another country.

Inextinguishable: Unquenchable, something that cannot be put out or stopped.

Insolent: Overbearing, insulting, arrogant and full of themselves.

Insurrection: Organized opposition to authority.

Junto: A group of persons joined for a common purpose. (Probably a variation of Junta).

Liberty: Freedom.

Mediate: To get involved with two or more quarreling people or *organizations* in order to help them reach an agreement.

Militia: A citizen army formed by citizens to serve in emergencies, usually dressed in civilian clothes.

Miscreant: Troublemaker.

Monarchs: People who rule over a kingdom or empire; supreme rulers.

Natural State: Untouched by civilization, living in the "wild."

Oppression: Unjust or extreme use of power.

Parasite: An organism living off another and giving nothing of value in return.

Passive: Lacking energy or will; inactive.

Petitions: Formal written requests or complaints, usually to ask for change.

Posterity: Future generations.

Privy Council: The private counselors selected by the monarch (king).

Prospered: To achieve economic success.

Province: A territory that has been around a long time and has history.

Rebellion: Usually an unsuccessful uprising. Defiance or revolt that is put down.

Reconciliation: To patch-up a friendship or give up something to end a disagreement.

Reformation, The: In Europe around 1517, religious life and how people participate in faith begins to change. Many people start rejecting the main religion of the time. Eventually, decades later, people looking to practice religious freedom find their way to the shores of North America.

Reign: To rule over subjects, usually with complete, unrestricted political power.

Repeal: To stop or reverse something through legislative power.

Repel: Resist, force away.

Representative: A person who speaks or acts for others.

Rigging: Ropes and chains used to work sails and other moveable parts of a ship.

Restitution: To pay for damage you caused.

Saltpeter: Mixed with sulphur and charcoal to create gunpowder.

Sanctuary: A place of safety and protection.

Sea stores: Supplies and food packed on a ship before starting a sea voyage.

Sedition: Resisting authority with the intent to hinder or overthrow the government.

Seized: To take with force.

Shipwright: Someone who builds ships.

Sorrow: Deep distress, sadness, or regret.

Sovereign: Independent political power.

Statutes: The ruling or judgment of a ruler.

Subject(s): Person(s) under the authority or control of a monarch.

Subvert: To corrupt someone's morals or existing law.

Suppression: Holding down or controlling someone or something.

Trespass: Entering onto someone's property without permission.

Tyrant: An absolute ruler who isn't concerned with law or freedoms for others.

Tyranny: A government where absolute power is held by one ruler.

Unification: To bring together.

Usurpation: To take something without legal authority.

Vile: Disgustingly bad; morally wicked.

Virtue: A personal trait or habit considered to be the best or righteous.

Wharf: A landing place or pier where ships may tie up and load or unload.

Withstood: To have successfully resisted something.

Ye: Old English term for "you" in certain types of writing.

Bibliography

(A partial list of the most easily available items.)

ARCHIVAL

Library of Congress, Rare Prints and Photographs Division
Library of Congress, Rare Book and Special Collections Division
National Archives on-line, United Kingdom

BOOKS

Adams, Samuel. *The Rights of Colonists.* Boston, 1772.

Boatner, Mark Mayo III. *Encyclopedia of the American Revolution.* Mechanicsburg, 1994.

Fischer, David Hackett. *Paul Revere's Ride.* New York, 1994.

Paine, Thomas. *Common Sense.* Philadelphia, 1776.

Langguth, A. J. *Patriots, the Men Who Started the American Revolution.* New York, 1989.

Martin, Joseph Plumb. *Narrative of a Revolutionary Soldier.* New York, 2001.

Savas, Theodore, and Dameron, J. David. *A Guide to the Battles of the American Revolution.* Savas Beatie 2006.

INTERNET

Officer, Lawrence H. *"Comparing the Purchasing Power of Money in Great Britain from 1264 to 2002."* Economic History Services, 2004, URL: http://www.eh.net/hmit/ppowerbp/

Index

Note: page numbers in *italic* indicate activities for the classroom